Make Telesales Work

Make Telesales Work

*Set up a successful telesales unit
and increase your profits*

STEPHEN KAYE

How To Books

Published by How To Books Ltd,
3 Newtec Place, Magdalen Road,
Oxford OX4 1RE, United Kingdom.
Tel: (01865) 793806. Fax: (01865) 248780.
email: info@howtobooks.co.uk
http://www.howtobooks.co.uk

First edition 2001

British Library Cataloguing in Publication Data.
A catalogue record for this book is available from
the British Library.

Edited by Peter Williams
Cover design by Shireen Nathoo Design
Cover image by PhotoDisc

Produced for How To Books by Deer Park Productions
Typeset by Kestrel Data, Exeter
Printed and bound by Cromwell Press Ltd, Trowbridge, Wiltshire

NOTE: The material contained in this book is set out in good
faith for general guidance and no liability can be accepted
for loss or expense incurred as a result of relying in particular
circumstances on statements made in the book. Laws and
regulations are complex and liable to change, and readers should
check the current position with the relevant authorities before
making personal arrangements.

Contents

Preface

The telephone is a highly available and extremely effective tool for people contact. There are increasing volumes of companies, from the very small to the international, which employ telephone executives and managers to increase their customer database and gain new clients, appointments and orders. Major companies without some form of telesales department are few.

Telesales departments can number from one to over one hundred personnel. Correctly managed, telesales is a highly cost-effective, low-overhead activity which can boost company sales and profit margins very, very effectively.

Telesales activity exists in a wide range of fields, from insurance to double-glazing, healthcare to advertising. National and regional newspapers use it to the full. Even charities now employ telesales managers to increase their incoming donations.

Throughout the western world, many companies are set up solely to contact people via the telephone, gaining contracts from businesses both small and large to make customer contact on their behalf.

The cost of a telesales call to a potential client or customer can be as little as 1p. The minimum cost of sending out a letter to a potential client in the UK, at time of writing, is 19p – some 94 per cent less! Telesales can therefore be far less expensive than mailing to possible buyers and the response is immediate.

Every keen salesperson wants to make fast and effective sales. The training and experience involved in making a telesales professional can be extensive but for many in the field it tends to be basic. Even with poor training, it is possible to make some sales, although any professional in the field would agree that it is good training, successful experience and competent management that counts.

There are key areas in the field of telesales which are covered in this book. Because they are so very important, they are mentioned more than once, and sometimes more than twice. Anyone involved in the telesales industry, whether in management or in the driving seat of a handset, needs to be particularly aware of these. Here's the first mention:

- Communications skills – communicating effectively, positively and clearly.

- Listening skills – taking note of what people are saying to them, really **hearing** it.

- The treatment of the customer/potential customer with respect, and as an intelligent individual.

- Qualification of prospects – just as it would be folly to try to sell snow to the Eskimos, or books to an illiterate, so the prospect must be qualified as able to use the products being offered.

- Last but not least – professionalism. That's really caring about doing it right, caring about what you actually produce, caring about your own standards.

At a conservative estimate, there are many tens of thousands of full- and part-time personnel engaged in the telesales industry in the UK alone. Each of these needs and wants good management in order to earn good commission. The high turnover of personnel in the field of telesales is attributed mainly to insufficient training and poor management.

- Managers and telesales executives alike want to increase the effectiveness of their role in this field.

- The telesales industry is currently expanding like never before.

- Postage costs remain prohibitive for the many, and e-commerce does not allow for person-to-person contact. Telephone contact is the viable option.

- As fuel costs increase, on-the-road sales personnel become fewer. Telephone costs, however, are coming down in cost regularly, with more options available from the independent telephone companies.

- Every telephone sales manager and his salespeople want to earn more money.

There are hit-and-miss ways of running any activity. Some work, most don't. The telesales industry abounds with 'techniques' and 'gimmicks', and while it is true that some of these do succeed, reading this book will give you well-researched fundamental ideas to guide your telesales management into the professional business it should be.

In this book, the term 'telesales executive' is used to describe the person who makes telesales calls. The reason for this is consistency of terminology and because, generally speaking, telesales personnel prefer to be called 'sales executives' – and rightly so.

Stephen Kaye
website:www.inyan.supunet.com
email: kaymex@inyan.netlineuk.net

Acknowledgements

Many thanks are due to Callco (The Call Company) of Torquay, and Eurobell South West for their input, expertise and assistance in the preparation of this book. Acknowledgement is also due to Beatrice, who tolerated and typed so patiently. Many thanks, too, to BT for allowing exerpts to be used from their *Talk Works* publication.

1

What is Telesales?

'Just imagine the impact we could have on your turnover without having to increase your workforce or the size of your premises! It's time to try a marketing method that really works!'

(Callco advertising slogan)

KNOW WHAT YOU'RE DOING

Companies sell their services and products using a variety of sales media. The most common of these are:

- the telephone
- direct mail
- fax
- television advertising
- video
- door-to-door sales people
- newspaper and magazine advertising
- local and national radio
- leaflet drops
- the internet
- e-mail
- posters and billboards
- shops
- vehicle advertising.

There are many more of course. This book deals with telesales as a medium for getting products and services known and sold, and as a sales tool, it is very effective.

WHAT IS TELESALES

Telesales is selling over the telephone. **Telemarketing** is marketing a product over the telephone. There is very little difference. Both utilise the telephone to get a product or service better known and better used, and to increase sales. **Direct mail** aims to increase sales of products and services via the letterbox. **TV advertising** aims to increase the use of goods and services through the screen. In the same way, the successful telesales executive gains sales over the telephone.

The first thing
The first thing to abolish completely from your mind is this:

> 'No one likes getting a telesales call.'

It is not true.

Nearly every business revolves around the frequent use of the telephone. Commerce today would grind to a halt without it. Almost 100 per cent of UK householders have a telephone. The reason for this is that they want to make and receive telephone calls. OK, I hear you say, but no one likes receiving a telesales call, do they? That is not strictly true. Actually, most people, either in business or at home, really do not mind, as long as a few basic conditions are met:

- The caller does not insult their intelligence by poor communication skills.

- The product or service being offered is **in some way relevant to their needs**.

If you think back to the last time that you received a telesales call that you did not enjoy, you will find that either one or both of the above conditions were not met. Of course, this does not mean to say that people are ecstatic about receiving telesales calls. Neither does it mean to say they will be particularly happy that someone called. However, it does mean that in order to have made an *acceptable* call, the above conditions must be met.

You have therefore already learned the following essential basics so far as telesales is concerned:

- Make certain that your telesales executives possess excellent telephone communication skills and use them.

- Ensure that your company only calls people who could use your products or services.

- Treat the people your company calls as intelligent individuals.

There are a number of other factors that will influence the effectiveness of your telesales executives, and later in the book we will look at these. However, for now, the above points are both essential and crucial to the success of any telesales or telemarketing operation, anywhere. Remember them and make good use of them.

Professionalism

Telesales is a **professional** sales activity. The use of professional telesales amounts to a remarkably effective sales tool. The success rate per 100 calls is far less than face-to-face, but more cost-effective. The reason for this is that using the telephone and effective telesales personnel, any company can eliminate many of the serious overheads of field sales.

To get 'in front of' the client, the field sales person would normally go through the following procedure:

- cold-calling;

- sending literature;

- following up the literature;

- gaining an appointment time and date;

- possibly having to reschedule at least once before getting in front of the client.

With an effective telesales department or team, the advantages are clear:

1. The call reaches the decision-maker and the caller immediately achieves a result.
2. This result can be negative or positive, but it is nearly always a definite outcome.
3. The result is clear, obvious and immediate.

The telesales executive's 'hit rate' from 100 telesales calls will be considerably less than the face-to-face field sales person's. Out of 100 calls the teleseller would make fewer sales. However, the overheads are far lower and the amount of time needed and taken to get to those 100 people is immensely less. This balance has worked in favour of telesales for many companies, especially with today's abundance and availability of telecommunication options.

The key differences between a telesales executive and a face-to-face sales person are:

- The telesales executive works more on tone of voice, i.e. aural signals.

- The field sales person works using face-to-face contact, body language and other complex human interactions.

Not just numbers

There are sales executives who will advise you that telesales is 'just a numbers game', and that you should 'employ really cheap staff, and when they've had enough, get some more'. These views are not only incorrect but also antiquated. They are un-professional too.

The intensive use of the telephone in any business activity is a profession engaged in by some of the finest salespeople around. Your company may have a service to sell, or a tangible product, or it could be that you merely want to get answers to questions or obtain valuable responses from a specific marketplace.

Whatever your business wants to achieve from the telephone, a professional sales approach is certainly the best and definitely the most effective way to do it.

As manager, your job is to ensure that your personnel achieve the result they need in the most professional manner. To be effective and professional yourself is equally important.

Image

Telesales has a poor image in the UK today. Ask any householder what they think of telesales calls and the reply will be more negative than positive. The main reason for this response is that the hiring, training and development of telesales executives has generally been to a poor standard to date. Many smaller telesales companies hire people on the promise of a 'fast buck', offering little training and demanding high results. This has led in turn to a generally low standard of telephone ethics.

You need to take effective steps to ensure that both you and your personnel are:

- fully trained;
- properly equipped;
- professionally able to do the job of selling over the telephone.

Motivation

Being at the forefront of commercial activities has never been easy. Telesales activity is very much in the vanguard because it entails that all-important initial approach. Sales personnel generally do not enter this field if they are looking for an easy life. They are usually highly motivated people, but will become demotivated on occasion. You should recognise the fact that your personnel are going to become demotivated from time to time and that you will have to motivate them again. This is a crucial part of your job as manager, and is covered more fully later in the book.

BEING EFFECTIVE – WHAT IT MEANS IN TELESALES

The keynotes of good management are:

- leading a team so that it produces well;
- motivating a team so that it produces well;
- developing a team to effectively achieve agreed production targets and objectives.

As someone in charge of a team that will become more effective, you will find yourself under constant pressure to meet targets.

Particularly in today's commercial climate, targets are an essential part of any management activity. There will always be stress on achieving targets, budgets and goals as cost-effectively as possible. This has to be done using a range of personal and managerial skills. Not the least of these skills are the ones you utilise to handle your personnel. Your personnel skills are some of the most important you will need. Often, managers forget the needs of the people for whom they are responsible. This can result in disaster.

Being effective in telesales means getting your personnel to get results that benefit your company, benefit the people you are working for, and benefit the customer.

Specifically, there are four areas, one or more of which may apply to your activity, where your well-managed telesales activity needs to show results. These are:

- getting orders for products and/or services;

- getting sales of products and/or services;

- gaining agreement for the contact to meet with a field sales representative;

- gaining start dates or delivery dates.

One or more of these areas of production will be how you measure the effectiveness of your telesales team. Later in this book, you will be invited to study the concepts of 'product' and 'production' very closely.

Being cost effective

Cost-effectiveness is an important aspect of any manager's duties, and the cost-effectiveness of your operation will determine how long you stay in business. One of the great advantages to tele-marketing and telesales is this: you are able to measure quite exactly not only the production, but also the cost of each telesales executive you have. This can be measured in such a way that you will always know how each of your personnel is doing, and just where you are making – or losing – profits.

UNDERSTANDING THE BASICS OF TELESALES MANAGEMENT

Every manager or would-be manager will already have, or be in the process of forming, their own personal philosophy of how to work with people. It is a 'life skill'. A life skill cannot be covered fully in a textbook because every person is different.

We all have a notion of one kind or other which tells us that good management is simply a matter of 'common sense'. The thing is – common sense is not very common at all. However, here are some ideas you can work with which are based upon successful telesales managers and their methods of building and working with a successful team of professional people.

The duties of an effective telesales manager:

- To get excellent production from their unit, department or business.

- To delegate tasks, therefore giving themselves more time to manage and develop the qualities of the personnel.

- Planning to achieve objectives.

- To manage problems – this does not mean solving all problems: rather it means delegating where necessary and placing problems exactly where they belong.

- To initiate and encourage ideas and innovation from the team.

- To develop and train teams to make existing personnel even more effective.

- To recruit and hire appropriate personnel.

- To motivate staff to perform to the best of their ability and to prevent demotivation.

Work

In any management or supervisory activity, it is important that you do not end up in a position where you are doing the work youself. This is particularly important in telesales management. You may have important deadlines to meet, or you may be way behind target and have to catch up. A test of a good manager is to show that they can achieve the necessary production from their team, utilising all resources as necessary. This may mean

temporarily hiring additional personnel or making overtime pay-
ments available on occasions.

Probably one of the worst things that you can allow to happen
to you as a telesales manager is this: you can drop into making the
calls yourself on a regular basis. An effective manager gets others
to do the work.

For example

A manager in a college was very kind, very sympathetic. Whenever any of his tutors or lecturers was not feeling too well or needed
some time off, they would ask him to cover their jobs. Because he
was unable to say 'no', and thought that his job was simply to 'make
certain the work was done', he would spend most of his week
covering the positions of those who were absent. He did not
understand that his job was to get others to do the work not do it
all himself. Eventually, no management was occurring at all and
the college had to be rescued by outside sources. The existing
tutorial and lecturing staff became disillusioned and eventually left.

> The strong manager holds lines firmly and gets others to
> do the work.

By all means, be an excellent example to your personnel
by demonstration and by showing 'how' as part of training your
personnel. It is important, however, that you do not end up by
doing the work yourself. If this happens you have ceased to be a
manager and have become a telesales executive instead. While
many managers do have a 'working' role, it is also important for
you to focus on establishing, building up and maintaining an
effective team under you. This doesn't mean that you never touch
the telephone. As a manager, you will gain the respect of your
personnel by demonstrating to them that not only can you do the
job, but that you can perform equally as well or better than they
can.

CASE STUDIES

Michael

Michael has a good history as a successful telesales executive. He
is now setting up his own office. He has little experience in

managing but feels he would both enjoy and excel with his own team under him. He has sold a number of different products using the telephone, and is confident that he has many of the skills and qualities necessary to be a good manager. Some of the points in this chapter have caused him to review his outlook, such as the emphasis on obtaining production from personnel. Michael, however, feels that he can study and find out about the things he does not know.

Sophie
Sophie has experience of working as a telesales executive and has worked for both 'good' and 'bad' managers. She is aware that on occasions she has tried to sell products and services to people where they were in no way relevant to their needs. Having gained greater experience now, she does recognise that the product or service she sells has to be pertinent in some way to the potential client's needs or wants.

Roger
Roger has his own property maintenance business. He has five people working for him. When he first started up, most of his business came from word of mouth (and still does). It also comes from canvassing houses and companies local to where he was working. Roger has a range of clients ranging from residential homes, hotels, some shops and private houses. Roger had tried direct mail in the past but has found that similar businesses to his use the same media and he wants to try something different. He has had the idea for some time that perhaps telesales is the answer, and would like to talk it over with someone he feels he could rely upon.

CHECKLIST

1. Poor telephone communication skills – give three examples that you have observed.

2. 'Doing the work yourself' – are you guilty of it? Recall three occasions when you 'did the work yourself' instead of getting the appropriate person to do it.

3. Take note this evening as you watch TV. How many of the products advertised are relevant to your own or your family's actual needs and desires? Is it a high or low percentage?

4. Write down three examples of selling an inappropriate product or service to someone.

2

Setting Up a Telesales Office

'Make yourself necessary to somebody.'
(Ralph Waldo Emerson)

Later in this book, there is information regarding office space, equipment, health and safety and other measures. However, for this chapter, let's look at the personnel who will be involved.

Questions

- Who do you hire?

- What would be their attributes and qualities?

- What is the right telesales manager like?

It is also important to look at some ideas about what it is you want your personnel to sell.

GETTING THE RIGHT TELESALES MANAGER – A PROFILE

It is outside the remit of this book to go into all the qualities of good managers and management training. However, there are key basics which should be fulfilled by anyone considering management, and these are covered in order that you can know where you are going as a manager, and the qualities which have to be present to run any activity effectively. At the end of the book, there are various texts and other works referenced which you may find to be useful.

Who makes a good telesales manager? What skills and attributes do you need to succeed? Are gender, experience and personality factors? All these things are important, but in this field an essential requirement for a successful telesales manager is to have been at least a reasonably successful telesales executive themselves. If as a manager you are dealing directly with telesales executives, then it is very important that you have as a first prerequisite a background of being able to deal with and sell to people using the telephone. It is important that you have a good understanding of the difficulties and problems that your telesales executives meet on a daily basis. You need to have been 'in the front line', so to speak.

Important strengths

Work through the list below to see where your strengths and weaknesses are:

1. Leadership skills	11. Personnel performance reviews
2. Listening skills	12. Managing your/others' stress
3. Time management skills	13. Budgeting
4. Management by objectives	14. Office layout
5. Goal setting	15. Finding and hiring personnel
6. Team building	16. Interviewing
7. Problem-solving	17. Training others
8. Decision-making	18. Communication skills
9. Motivation	19. Patience
10. Gaining new business	20. Telephone selling skills

FINDING THE RIGHT TELESALES EXECUTIVE – A PROFILE

Who do you hire and what should they be like?

The most successful telesales people ('telesales executives') are those who **already have a successful record of accomplishment in sales**. A major positive attribute is confidence. Confidence comes with experience, of course, and there is no better way to gain experience on the telephone than by making many sales calls. The confidence that any good telesales executive possesses usually comes from having made sales in the past. Confidence also comes from having dealt with difficult and/or rude customers, and there is something to be said for the skills often needed to make contact with the right person despite tough and exacting receptionists and secretaries. As more people use the telephone to make contact with potential customers or clients, it gets harder to get through to the important people who do make the decisions. Those who have developed the tenacity, drive and communications skills to do this repeatedly are going to be the best personnel. So look out for experienced sales personnel who still have plenty of drive.

Figure 1 shows some examples of personnel advertisements you may find useful.

EXPERIENCED SUCCESSFUL TELESALES EXECUTIVES REQUIRED

Do you have a successful record of accomplishment in professional telephone sales?

If so, we would be very interested to speak to you.

- **Fully qualified leads**
- **An excellent working environment**
- **A salary and bonus scheme commensurate with your skills and experience**
- **Full product training**

For the right people, we'll listen to your needs and offer you a package you cannot refuse!

Contact me in confidence at:
Ringaround, 1, The High Street, Anytown, Anywhere.
Tel: 01111 01234 Fax: 01111 01236 E-mail: theboss@ringaround.com

---

Telesales opportunities
£10–£12k basic, ote £16k and extra benefits

Why Telesales?

Telephone sales offer you an opportunity to take control of your future and shape your career in sales. The skills you will acquire alongside your personal attributes of self-motivation, intelligence and a strong desire to succeed will guarantee your future sales success, either within an internal or within an external sales environment. These are not temporary positions or hourly jobs, but a real opportunity for a long and successful career in professional business-to-business sales.

You can e-mail us, fax us, telephone us, or write to us.

The Telesales Company Ltd
Tel: 01234 567891 Fax: 01234 123456 E-mail: thetel@ephoneco.co.uk

---

Fig. 1.   Examples of personnel advertisements.

Points to look for
1. First, a good telephone manner is essential. This includes a good speaking voice, clarity and good diction.

2. In some ways, a good telephone manner **could** include being a long-term resident of the area, or having a local dialect or accent. If you will be making mainly local calls, this may help you to relate better with the people in the local community. Local people know the area, they know the people, and they have something in common with the person at the other end of the telephone line, something to talk about. This will breed an affinity and assists in striking up a relationship within the first 30 seconds, which is vital. Local knowledge is always an asset.

3. A good telephone sales executive needs to have an amenable and approachable manner. They also need to be able to speak to people in a way that encourages them to speak back.

4. The right telessales executive needs the vital ability to listen to other people. It is of no use to ask the right question and then fail to wait for the answer. This is a vital skill because if a telesales executive cannot listen, then they will not get their questions answered. Good questioning and listening are the route to finding out about your potential customers' needs and wants. Only then can you sell your products and services effectively. A telesales executive who spends five minutes talking to your customer, telling them what a great product you have on offer and not listening to the person at the other end of the telephone will not sell. They will not understand the customer's needs.

The successful telesales executive should be able to learn and understand all the salient points of a product or service. They should be able to impart these to the potential customer without the need for a script. Scripts, generally, are not recommended. Some type of format for 'leading' a customer through what you want your telesales executives to say, including all the key benefits and selling points, is important as a guide. But directly reading through a script over the telephone sounds wooden and does not allow for honest listening and proper communication. Both the seller and the potential buyer must be 'in communication', meaning that both of them are listening, talking and understanding.

Good salesmanship has been described by a leading sales person as 'leading them on a journey that they don't know they are on'. A good sales person will sell you something without you being particularly aware that they are selling, almost conversationally. At the end of the conversation, the sales person and the buyer will make a joint decision about the product and go on from there.

Observe

- Think about a time when you have been 'sold' something by a sales person and you will see that you have been 'led on a journey which you didn't know you were on' – the experience was natural, easy and cooperative.

- Watch your most experienced sales person. Note how their speaking style is conversational.

Face-to-face sales are much easier for the professional sales person because they can see the customer's responses fully. They can 'read' the situation so much better, and there are things in the environment which can be used to open up or take forwards conversation. None of these things is available to the telesales executive. That is why it is so important that telesales personnel are good listeners. Unless the telesales executive listens, they will not know whom they are talking to and therefore will not be able to enter into dialogue to establish the customer's needs. The result being that they will not sell to that person.

Product knowledge can be taught, as can computer literacy and some sales skills, but the basics of listening skills have to be there already.

Basic attributes of a good telephone sales executive:
1. Good telephone manner
2. An amenable and friendly approach to people.
3. High quality listening skills.

Important points to look for in a telephone sales executive:
1. Experience in sales.
2. Confidence.
3. Drive to succeed.

Not all of your personnel are going to be top high-flyers. That's OK – as long as your low-flyers are on target. Most telesales managers have a basic expectation in terms of production, and if any individual wants to exceed that by leaps and bounds, earning a lot of money in the process, that's up to them.

GETTING STARTED

'Nothing is ever as pristine, as determined, as dynamic, and clear in its vision of the future, as it is at the moment of its creation.'

(Archie Hernandez)

Where do you want to pitch yourself in the market?

If you're part of a business that is setting up its own telesales department, then you don't have to make those decisions. The company will have already established that, and your products or services are already defined. You just have to get on with the business of marketing and selling them. **But what if you're setting up a new telesales business? Who are you going to call? Where do your clients come from? Moreover, on what types of product or service are you going to concentrate?**

First things first, though. Decide where you want to pitch yourself in the market. Which type of products or services do you want your company to market and sell? Which types of business are right for you and your company? Whom do you want to call? Which of these would it be:

- large companies?
- small companies?
- individuals?
- the self-employed?
- men?
- women?

- specific income levels?
- home owners?

Areas of business

Here are just a few examples of product and service fields, any of which you may wish to become involved in:

- construction
- building
- surveying
- soft drinks
- financial services
- insurance
- medical cover
- domestic central heating
- environmentally-friendly products and services
- office furniture
- advertising
- newspapers
- books
- car and garage
- computers
- insulation
- charities
- software.

Ask yourself

- Would you be looking for long-term relationships with your clients?
- On the other hand, would you be looking for a number of short-term one-off contracts for immediate promotional needs?

- What size of company is it best for your business to work with? (If you're a three-man band, better leave the multinationals for now.)

Tip: Concentrate on working for companies that are a similar size to your own operation.

When you've formulated some idea of the type of goods or services your business would be most successful with, it will be primarily your role to seek out the decision-makers in that field and approach them with ideas and a costing for the services you can offer. Some companies pay by the quantity of leads you supply to them on a monthly basis, if it's a longer-term contract. Others will pay a standard flat rate throughout the contract. You may find that some businesses will require your services for a special promotion, and intensive use of your personnel is required for three or four days only.

Some important points

- Remember that companies will not continue a contract with you if the results are not forthcoming.

- In addition, telephone bills and personnel wages are all commitments that have to be met regardless of your levels of success.

- Ensure that you are confident you can achieve the targets worked out with the companies with which you choose to do business.

- Are the companies you work for in a position to pay you? The outlay in wages and telephone costs will be the major outgoing, and these have to be offset against guaranteed income from your clients. There are always bad payers. It is therefore prudent to take as many steps as possible to ensure payment is guaranteed for the services you deliver.

- Any company that uses the telephone a lot should be able to negotiate a good rate with their service provider. Telephone companies normally have set rates up to a certain range and you will need to check with yours to determine the current rates. As there are now a number of different telephone companies, it can pay you to shop around to get the best rates for the quantity of calls you will be making.

The office and its equipment are fully covered in Chapter 8. Initially, however, make certain that the premises you operate from are appropriate in terms of lighting, heating and ventilation and are easily accessible. It is also wise to check if there is likely to be any difficulty in putting in extra telephone lines and adding to the existing space.

CASE STUDIES

Michael
Michael has realised, after reading the lists above, that he needs more knowledge in the area of finding and hiring good personnel. He enrols on an appropriate evening management course at his local college, realising he has to be more pragmatic in his approach to running his own telesales business, or else it will fail. As his essential interest is in the field of computing, he thinks he will opt to sell services and/or products for this type of company, but he also has knowledge about the building industry. Therefore, he is going to utilise this by adding that field to his portfolio. He begins his research on companies which will be about the same size as the one he is setting up, doing all he can to ensure they are solid, solvent companies.

Sophie
Sophie recognises that she is already a confident telesales executive with an excellent telephone manner, although she realised she could improve her listening skills. She recognises that she is often so eager to sell the product that she does not always listen fully, thereby missing valuable information from the client which could expand her sales.

Roger
Roger has noticed an advertisement in the local press, placed by Michael's new business. He gets in touch. Michael arranges an appointment with Roger and his partner to see if they can do business together.

CHECKLIST

1. What essential attributes should a telesales executive possess? Does your view differ from the above? In what way?

2. Go through the lists above. What percentage of the qualities and attributes of a good telesales manager do you possess already? Work out how you can improve upon the number of attributes you have.

3. What type of products or services would you sell over the telephone? Who do you think you would contact to gain contracts for this?

3

How to Make Yourself a Really Effective Manager

> 'The great managers are the ones who challenge the existing complacency and who are prepared to lead their teams forward towards a personal vision.'
>
> (Gerard M. Blair)

THE SINGLE MOST EFFECTIVE THING YOU CAN DO

There is much advice that can be given to the new manager on the subject of being effective and getting results.

However, probably the **single most positive and effective thing you can do as a manager** is to understand fully exactly what it is that your unit, department, company and organisation is supposed to be producing. That may sound absurd – 'Doesn't everyone know that?' you may say. It can be surprising to find out just how many line managers and others in charge of business activities fail to clarify exactly this issue.

- What should your activity be producing?

- What result are you aiming for?

- What is it that you as manager should be producing?

> **Product: a definition**
> 'That which is produced by any action, operation, or work: a production: the result.'

Example

John Smith makes and sells shoes. A customer comes in and orders new shoes – specific type, specific colour and, of course, a very specific fit. John Smith makes the shoes, taking care to use high-quality materials of the specified type and colour. Having measured the customer's feet, he then makes the shoes to the right fit. When the customer comes to collect his shoes, they fit and the customer is pleased with the way they look and feel. He is happy, and so gives John Smith money. The customer then takes the shoes away.

- Had John Smith not completely finished the shoes, the customer would not have paid for them

- Had John Smith not provided the customer with high-quality shoes, had they been poorly stitched or scratched, the customer would not have paid for them.

- Had John Smith never got around to contacting the customer to tell him his shoes were ready, or had the customer never taken his shoes, then John Smith would never have been paid for them.

So all the factors listed above need to be in place in order for it to be said that John Smith had fully produced a pair of shoes, and that the production of that pair of shoes had benefited his company or activity in some positive manner.

DOING WHAT YOU SHOULD BE DOING

Now let's look at the product which your telesales department is supposed to be producing.

Here's where you do some work

Work out exactly what your telesales department or organisation/company/unit produces. That's your **product**.

When you think you have done this (it may take several tries before you get it exactly) check your result against the following:

- Is it of value? Is it something that others would be willing to pay for, or for which they would exchange valuable goods?

- Is it complete in its own right? Is it complete enough to have real value to someone? Does it need further work?

- Is it of a high enough quality? Does it meet the laid down standards for that type of item or service? Is it shoddy? Is it the best your company can do?

- Are there existing means of getting this product to the consumer? What are they exactly?

- What thing of value is it exchangeable for? How does this exchange occur?

- Can you measure the production of this service or product? How?

- When your product definition measures up against the above, write it down.

Your product definition

Put it on a large poster in large lettering. Refer to it repeatedly. Read it, refine it, study it, make sure it is emblazoned in the front of your mind. Ensure that every one of your actions as manager aligns with it. If you do this, you will be doing the single one thing that will hold you firm and take your department or business forward more than any other single action will. Think and act in terms of the above product, and as long as you do not make any major mistakes, you will have it made.

It is fair to say that the chief activity anyone will expect from you and your department is effective production. This production will, of course, be set against budgets and targets for the area. It may be someone else who will set the overall budgets, but it is you who will have to see to it they are met, and, of course, you who will take the credit (or the discredit) for the outcomes of your efforts.

Some examples of results in the field of telesales, which are often erroneously thought of as being products, are:

- number of telephone calls made (it is **effective** contacts you are looking for, and the positive result of that telephone contact);

- amount of time spent on the telephone (the amount of time spent talking does not necessarily reflect any gain for the company);

- total number of employees engaged upon telephone activity (although this can eventually lead to a lot of production, it is by no means any guarantee of such);

- items which are produced and not paid for;

- items which are not handed over to the customer;

- undelivered items.

Depending on what it is that your executives are supposed to be producing, the wording will be different. Here are some ideas of how you could word the product definition for different types of activity:

- 'Appointments' could be fully expressed as: 'A confirmed appointment with a qualified potential client, correctly recorded for invoicing and passed on to Smith & Sons' (or whoever the appropriate person is – it may be the client's field sales rep, for example).

- Getting orders for products and/or services could be fully expressed as: 'an order for [product/s], which meets company profit and sales margins, and which is fully confirmed by fax/telephone/letter – passed on to the appropriate manager for processing'.

- Gaining start dates or delivery dates could be fully expressed as: 'Start/delivery date/s given to the customer, fax confirmation received back, and date/s, material/s or service/s fully logged and recorded by appropriate manager'.

The full wording may vary immensely according to exactly what it is you are expecting your telesales executives to produce. The key criterion is that the product definition must reflect the whole product, as it should be delivered to either the next person to work with it, or to the customer.

MEASURING YOUR PRODUCTION

Once you can easily and fully define exactly what it is that your activity should be producing, it should be only a small step to work out how to measure it. In the example above, John Smith was producing high-quality, well-fitting shoes. All John would need to do to measure his output would be to graph the number of pairs of high-quality, well-fitting shoes he produced **and was paid for** every week, or every month, and draw a graph to show this. (In time, he would reach a ceiling whereby he could produce no more shoes in the time available, at which point he would need to employ and train more personnel to keep his production moving in the right direction.) One of the reasons that small (and large) businesses fail is that they do not effectively recruit and train more personnel to maintain their production in an upward curve.

When you can define and measure the right product/s that your activity is supposed to be producing, then you can steam right ahead, knowing exactly what it is you are aiming for. Not only that, but:

- you are able to recognise things that should not be produced;
- you can align all your own and your telesales executives' efforts towards greater production;
- measuring production and drawing graphics to show where your team is going will be easy;
- explaining to your team and to any higher management exactly what is occurring in your department will be a pleasure, not a chore!

How to draw a graph which tells you what you need to know

Let's draw a graph that is designed to show the weekly production of a telesales executive over a one-month period. For this you will need:

- a sheet of A4 graph paper;
- a black pen;
- a pencil.

1. Along the bottom (short side) of the graph paper, write in the week-ending dates of the weeks of the month.
2. Work out both the minimum and the maximum amount of products likely in any given week for that telesales executive.

(This can be worked out from experience and data, or if no data are to hand, can be realistically estimated.)

3. Count the number of horizontal thick lines on the sheet, and divide this figure into the highest figure you have in the previous step.

4. Each thick line going across will now be equal to the figure worked out in the last step. Number them appropriately, so that by the time you reach the top line, it will be equal to the maximum amount of products you could expect that telesales executive to achieve.

Figure 2 shows an example. You will now be able to easily assess how that telesales executive is progressing on their expected production per week/month.

Remember, one telesales executive achieving less production one week than they did in the previous week does not make a catastrophe. It is always wise to look at the bigger picture before you decide to panic. View the production graphs of any of your executives over say, a three- or a four-week period, then you can establish not only how they are producing week to week, but what kind of **trend** their production is on. It may take a dip mid-month, but if the overall **trend** is upwards, there's no need to panic!

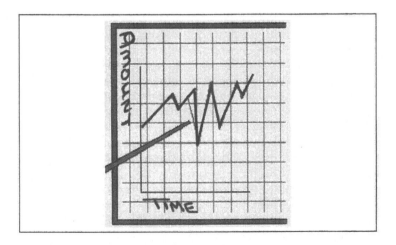

Fig. 2. Example of a graph.

CASE STUDIES

Michael
Michael works hard to truly define exactly what it is that he and his sales executives are supposed to be producing, in order that he can be as specific as possible about his activity as manager. Realising that he has not fully crystallised this before, he comes up with many things that do not stand too much scrutiny. Eventually, he arrives at a definition of his products that he is happy with, and which can be measured statistically. 'Sales on behalf of the client' now seems an insufficiently worded product, given his new learning, and he wonders how he ever managed with such a scant definition of what he was supposed to be doing.

Sophie
Sophie finds that fully defining exactly what she is supposed to produce is tremendously helpful. She has her product graphed, so that she can see exactly how she is progressing towards her weekly target and where she is falling down and needs to improve.

Roger
Roger meets Michael, and they discuss the type of response that will be needed if Roger is to lay out hard-earned money for Michael's services. Roger finds that Michael is keen to arrive at an exact wording for the products that Roger expects from the company.

CHECKLIST

1. Ask five people (friends, colleagues) exactly what it is they are supposed to produce. Do they know?

2. Ask several people all engaged in the same activity what it is they are supposed to produce. Are they all thinking along the same lines?

3. Observe some simple tasks which people do for work. Try to define exactly what is their final product.

4. How 'excellent' is your training for management? Do you need to improve upon it?

5. Review the positive side of your experience with people. Do you consider that you have enough positive experience to cope with the problems that will be thrown at you as a manager?

4

How to Make Your Telesales Team Really Effective

COMMUNICATION

We spend a major part of our lives talking, listening and responding to the people around us. Good communication doesn't 'just happen'. When it doesn't happen – which is much of the time – our tendency is to blame the other person or simply accept that the conversation was somehow destined to fail.

There is another way. That is to take personal responsibility for the quality of our conversations. If we put our minds to it, we all have the power to influence every conversation for the better.

The ability to carry on effective conversations is, in fact, the principle enabling skill of life. In other words, it lies behind just about every other life skill. If this is true, then surely it makes sense to be as good as we can at having conversations that work out for the best.

Communication skills

Why do some sales calls work well while others fail? Why do some sales people become misunderstood so often? While nearly every sales person agrees that the way we communicate is important, it is odd how little attention we devote to developing our talents in this vital area. Unfortunately, communication skills are not often taught at school, leaving many people, even sales people, badly armed for the battles to be fought in the sales arena.

Let's take conversation. Think of conversation as an activity that has the aim of creating shared understanding. At any particular moment, one person is trying to be understood and the other person is trying to understand. Dialogue, then, involves two roles, both of which include talking and listening.

First, there is the role of the person who wants to be understood as they tell a story, communicate a message or explain a point of view. Let's call this role the 'Teller'.

The job of the Teller is to engage and hold the attention of the other person – and to make it as easy as possible for the other person to get the main points clear in his or her mind. The person who is absorbing the story, message or point of view plays the other role in dialogue. Let's call this role the 'Understander'.

The job of the Understander is to work hard at really understanding what the Teller is saying. This not only involves listening carefully, but also asking for more information and checking their understanding as the conversation goes along.

Communication and telesales

In telephone sales work, it becomes more difficult to communicate because there is no body language for the person communicating to gauge what effect their communication is having upon the listener. The person communicating down the telephone is, in fact, half-blind, so must develop a very keen sense of gauging the reactions of others. This is done by listening and noting reactions to your message by the pauses, tone of response or lack of it, and a million other almost intuitive ways by which a professional experienced telesales executive will know which way the conversation is headed. A good telesales executive will learn to act quickly to maintain the other's interest level – assuming they have been interested initially.

Good communicators know how important it is to actively engage the other person's attention and get them involved in the conversation right from the start. Left on our own, our attention often turns inward. In effect, we talk to ourselves. We can get lost in our thoughts. It can take quite an effort to redirect this attention towards someone else, especially if we already have some important things on our mind. This is why it is so essential for the person who is opening communication to 'hook' the other's attention at the beginning of a conversation.

When you open a newspaper or magazine, what catches your attention is the headline. Headlines are extremely useful because they tell you what the following article is all about. You can utilise the same concept in sales calls to focus the attention around specific topics, points and issues. Good telephone sales people make sure they communicate clearly by including the right balance of ingredients in their conversations. They realise how important it is to fill in the picture with pertinent and interesting facts about their products or services.

If you fail to provide the person at the other end of the telephone line with concrete ideas and information, they'll simply fill in the gaps for themselves. Often enough, their assumptions will be wrong, or at least distorted.

> Make your details concrete and specific, as opposed to vague and general.

Scripts

Scripts are a good, workable method of ensuring that your telesales people are getting across to the potential customer all the key points in as short a time as possible. However, few people can read from a script without it sounding just like that – reading from a script. To the person at the other end of the telephone line it becomes a total turn-off, and it demonstrates in an instant to that person just how uninterested the caller really is in talking to them. Anyone reading this book has had such calls him or herself. The response of many people to listening to a 'scripted' telephone call is to want to interrupt and end the telephone call as soon as possible. Reading rotely from a script is almost rude. If your telesales team cannot study a script, understand and absorb the key points in it, and communicate the message in a natural way down the telephone then you may have to reconsider the training and attributes of that teleseller.

Points to remember

It has been said many times that when we speak, we communicate our attitude, confidence and competence across the telephone line. Exhibiting telephone excellence can not only be enjoyable, but can reap you incredible rewards, too.

- Be expressive.
- Be yourself.
- Speak as you would to a friend, or perhaps more appropriate, a business colleague.
- Be personal, not impersonal.
- Smile. Even if the person at the other end of a telephone line can't see you smile, it still conveys sincerity and enthusiasm.
- Volume is important. Use an appropriate volume. Speak as if the person you are talking to were two or three feet away.

- Be clear as you talk. Speak crisply. Avoid slurring syllables or trailing off at the end.

- Check out your voice speed. Your speech speed can indicate your attitude. The ideal rate is 150 – 160 words per minute. If you speak faster, the person you are trying to sell to may doubt your credibility. If you speak any slower, you may bore your listener.

- Use positive language. The words and phrases you use will shape another's opinion and image of you. These can and usually do affect whether the other person will decide to co-operate with you.

- Use your first and last name to identify yourself.

TRAINING

Train your people

A full week's training would be the absolute minimum for any new telesales executive before you would 'let them loose' on the telephone. It is important for them to get to know team members, get to grips with the products they are selling, possibly even working with the product itself in some form to really increase familiarity and product knowledge. Some companies even send their new telesales executives out with field sales reps to gain field knowledge. Working in the production department can increase product reality considerably. The methods used within the tele-sales department may also be unfamiliar, even if your personnel have a lot of experience in telesales. This can include use of office computers and the methods you wish to use or be used for recording and logging calls, orders, etc.

Until a new telesales executive is fully trained and fully familiar with the product and the way your company sells, you do not want them to be under pressure from targets. So ease off with target setting until you are certain they know how the job in your company, how the products and how the team, all work. Then, you can ease over onto targets. This would normally take two months.

There is no substitute for truly understanding the product you are trying to sell – no substitute at all. All the 'sales skills' in the world will not make up for a lack of understanding on your telesales executives' part of your company's product or service.

Of course, the nature of telesales is not to have a substitute for sales representatives. Nevertheless, a good understanding of the company services and products will enable your telesales people to be more confident about dealing with any response.

MOTIVATION AND INCENTIVES

How does a good manager go about motivating their telesales executives?

Motivation means different things to different people, because all people are motivated in different ways.

Your essential task as manager is to keep your people motivated. This includes having a laugh, praising them when appropriate, the 'carrot and stick' approach – whatever it takes. Your personnel need to know that when they're doing their jobs properly, when things are good and when they are not succeeding.

Personnel also need to know that you can be a tough manager. However, they also need to know that you will understand their own individual needs. Motivation is different for everyone. Some people come to work for money; others come to work because they just like coming to work. The person who comes to work purely for money is not particularly interested in whether they like the job or the environment – they just wants to get on and earn money. There are as many different reasons for coming to work as there are people.

Management through fear does not work (e.g. 'Get the results I demand or you are out of a job'). It serves no purpose to become feared as a manager. Your personnel are not only your greatest asset; they are the tools of your job and the energy of the company. Without happy, effective, contented personnel, nothing is possible.

The management of people is very individual. There is a wealth of books on the subject of people management, and some excellent references on managing are detailed at the end of this book. Each individual has a slightly different style of management and you have to work out for yourself how to incorporate good management basics into your personal style and personality.

Telesales is an intense activity. Sitting in the same place all day, every day, selling is intense. Therefore, what the telesales executive does not need is an intense manager. Follow the pointers above and you should have it about right.

The management style of a good telesales manager should be the same as the telephone style of a good telesales executive:

- a good communication manner;

- an amenable approach;

- a high-quality listener.

JUST HOW DO YOU MOTIVATE OTHERS?

There are several important points to understand and remember whenever you are dealing with your personnel:

- Everyone likes admiration. Even those who say they don't.

- Sales people particularly enjoy admiration.

- Appreciation is important.

- Acknowledgement of our actions is important.

All employees like to know how they are doing in the eyes of the company, and how they can perform better. For above-average performance, personnel normally would enjoy some form of recognition. This fuels the process of self-motivation.

First thing in the morning, have a meeting and get agreement as to what each telesales executive is going to achieve for that day. Each member of the team will pledge what they intend to achieve for that day, and this activity in itself can have an uplifting effect upon anyone who is feeling down.

It is important not to focus in on anyone who appears to be in a negative mood, or down, as this can in turn have a negative effect upon the rest of the team.

If you feel down, take a break and don't come back until you're ready to do your work. Clear your head, have some fresh air – whatever it takes.

It is important during meetings which are designed to motivate never to draw attention to any particular person who appears to be demotivated or feeling 'down'. It is far better to have a quiet one-to-one with that person and discuss any issues they may have on their mind. If anyone seems isolated for any reason, take them aside – do not discuss things with them in front of the others.

Aside from personal problems or difficulties, you can also ask them if they need more training. Is there any problem at work? Ask questions of your personnel to locate the problems before they get out of hand. This is important for two reasons:

- If that individual continues to feel low, it will markedly affect their production for the day.

- One negative person can very quickly demotivate and affect the whole team.

Positives
There are many ways to motivate your telesales team. Here are some positive examples:

- promotions;
- 'outstanding achievement' lists;
- cash bonuses for good suggestions;
- employee of the week/month/quarter/year;
- raises in salary;
- prizes;
- company merchandise;
- letter from the boss (framed?);
- plaque award.

Negatives
There are also negative ways to motivate your personnel:

- fear ('do your job or you're out');
- starting bonuses/rewards at a level of production that means only a few will be able to even enter the scheme, for example 'the first ten orders/appointments do not carry a bonus';

- praising and acknowledging exceptional results only;
- motivating the team but not the individual.

More examples of positive ways to motivate personnel would include:

- excellent communication with each individual to ascertain his or her needs and using that to motivate;
- measuring your personnel against their own previous attainments, not against other personnel. That way, you set them up to improve their own performance on an ongoing basis. There will always be unbeatable top telesales executives in any group, so do not make the mistake of setting all against the highest achievers. It will be demotivating for those who cannot make that grade;
- motivate by satisfying individual needs;
- unannounced rewards for effort/ideas/contribution;
- don't forget that effort must be praised as well as achievement.

CASE STUDIES

Michael

Michael is working in earnest to be an excellent manager of his own telesales team. He has drawn up a full regime of training for the six telesales executives under him, including the basic points of telesales. This especially includes getting them fully trained on the products he will be selling. Most of those he has hired are experienced telesales executives, but he is making a determined effort to really get to know each of them, so that he can establish just what their personal needs and drives are to ensure he is motivating each one appropriately. Michael has a small office so that he will be able to have private meetings with the individuals under him where necessary.

He is working out various ways of rewarding members of his team, bearing in mind the points he has read.

Sophie

Sophie has noticed that she uses her script often. Listening to herself, she hears that she sounds a little 'robotic' at times. She has decided to continue to utilise the script, but to work on changing some of the phraseology to words which she would normally use herself, so that she sounds more natural. 'I never did like using some of those words. I know some much simpler ones which feel more comfortable for me to use.' She had discussed with her manager the important areas of the products she is selling so that she is fully familiar with these, and so that she will not 'fumble' for words when she is asked a 'difficult' question.

Roger

Roger is pleased at the outcome of his meeting with Michael. A contract has been agreed which means that Michael will supply Roger with confirmed appointments for Roger's sales representative to see regarding property maintenance. Roger's business will pay for these appointments regardless of whether or not his salesman manages to convert the appointments into hard orders. Rogers' company has asked for up to 15 of these per week and will pay monthly. If there are less than five appointments over any given three-week period over the next three months, Roger has the right to terminate the contract without further notice. He is also going to arrange to run a mini training session with Michael's telesales executives later, so that they can get any queries resolved and offer his services more professionally.

CHECKLIST

1. Today, observe the way you communicate with others.

2. Recall a time when you sold a product easily and without effort. How much of what you achieved was due to being motivated?

3. Think about different managers you have had. For whom did you like working? What means did they use to motivate their staff?

5

Learning Telesales Techniques

(PRODUCT) KNOWLEDGE IS EVERYTHING

Nigel was a good salesman but he 'lived on adrenaline'. Never able to really absorb information or study, Nigel took the main points in during his product training, and very little else. He decided to 'bluff his way through' to the customers with anything he didn't know. Consequently, Nigel told many lies and gave out much inaccurate information during his brief sales career with Mark & Sons. Nigel eventually had to leave the company. Why? Although he did get good sales figures, these were always taken off his totals at the end of the month because of later client complaints and promises being broken. We've all probably known a 'Nigel' at some time – determined to impress, never standing still, initial good sales figures – but essentially just plain stupid, because there's no long-term results if your personnel do not really understand the products they are trying to sell.

> There is no substitute for a true understanding of the product you are selling – none at all.

All the 'sales skills' in the world will not make up for a lack of understanding on your telesales executives' part of your company's product or service.

Most companies run excellent training for their sales people. When your team are selling products and services, the client you are selling for will normally be very pleased to offer you all the help they can in order to ensure that your team have a really good understanding of the products and services they are selling. You should find that you could even get your telesales executives to undertake training at the offices of the client, either that or they will come to you. Even if the product appears quite simple and straightforward, it is surprising what queries the potential customer can come up with.

THE MOST IMPORTANT TELEPHONE TECHNIQUE OF ALL

People who are new to sales and many who have been sales people all their lives can have many questions abut 'telesales technique'. What is it? Can we live without it? Is it magic? Can anyone do it?

So what are the answers? A study of the various 'sales skills' and 'techniques' that abound today will show that the answers may all be classified into three main areas:

1. methods of getting another's attention;
2. methods of gaining agreement and cooperation;
3. listening skills.

It is not magic; no, a telephone sales executive cannot live without it; and no it is not something anyone can do. 'Telesales techniques' can be grouped under one heading – that of 'communications skills'. Again, it can be seen just how very important it is to any telesales manager or telesales executive to have excellent telephone communications skills. This has been well covered in Chapter 4, but in an attempt to demystify the subject of sales techniques, it is well worth reiterating.

Real telesales technique

Real telephone sales technique is simply this: excellent telephone communications skill. There is a very wide range of gimmicks, phrases and stances that any sales person can take, all of which may help to get a potential customer to sit up and take note. However, where telephone sales are concerned, the skill that counts more than any other is excellent telephone communications skill.

It is important to recognise that different people can achieve different results, depending on to whom they are speaking. There are occasions (particularly those where the telesales executive is dealing with older, more mature people), where an element of maturity and gravitas are appropriate. Such occasions may include the sale of burglar alarms, security installations and some types of insurance. On these occasions, a younger person may not fare as well as a mature sounding telephone executive.

ASKING THE RIGHT QUESTIONS

Qualifying the customer

Before a client or customer will buy, they have to be **qualified**. 'Qualified' is very important as it lets you know whether it is worth proceeding with the steps to attempt a sale. 'Qualified' means the following:

- the person or company could use your product or service;

- they are able to afford your product.

For example:

- Businesses need computers, computer supplies, office supplies, some insurance, some pensions, personnel, coffee machines, building maintenance, telephone services, lighting.

- Businesses (generally) do not need television and audio equipment, personal healthcare and weekly deliveries of frozen fish.

- Residential property owners need carpet and upholstery cleaning, home improvement services, home shopping.

Here's an old example that has been used on every sales executive I've known. Older, experienced field sales people use it to intimidate younger sales people.

'Here, sell me this box of matches!' says the senior sales person, handing the more inexperienced sales person a box of matches. The younger sales person then proceeds to try to force the other into accepting the box of matches, attributing all manner of qualities, advantages and benefits to the box of matches, ranging from the sublime to the ridiculous. Eventually, the younger sales person begins to offer discounts on the cost of the box of matches, panicking because he is being rebuffed at every turn by the other's objections to buying. Most of the time, the senior sales person either 'allows' the other to 'sell' him the matches, or makes a point of not buying to demonstrate his resistance and toughness. It's a hackneyed drill, usually serving to highlight nothing other than the ebullience of senior sales people and the naivety of younger ones.

However, it does serve as an excellent example of the previous point about qualifying the prospect. In the panic to 'sell', sales people often forget to continue to qualify their prospect, and forget to continue to ask intelligent, pertinent questions!

Ask pertinent questions

Suppose you are the younger sales person in the drill. You could probably achieve a sale merely by intelligent and pertinent questioning:

- Do you smoke?

- Does anyone close to you smoke?

- Do you collect matchboxes?

- Do you ever need a naked flame? Perhaps in the house? In the garage?

- Do you use candles in the home?

- Have you ever found yourself without a light? Does your lighter ever run out at inconvenient times?

- Does your ignition switch on the cooker ever fail?

- Is there any way that a box of matches around the home would be of some use to you?

Perhaps most pertinent of all:

- 'Don't you find it infuriating when you need a light and you just can't lay your hands on one? Here, take these for a few pence and throw them in the glove compartment – you'll be glad you did one day!'

You get the picture.

Make sure the customer is qualified

If your company does not buy in or obtain its own leads for potential customers who are already qualified, it will be up to your telesales executives to qualify the person right at the beginning of the telephone call. Just as it would be pointless (as well as a total waste of time and money) to telephone flat owners to find out if they would like to buy a garden shed, it is folly to embark upon a sales pitch without first establishing if the person has a need for your product, to say nothing of the finances to pay for it.

You would not consider the following 'qualified':

- You would not be able to sell milk to a dairy.

- If a person were unemployed and receiving benefits, offering mortgage services would probably be a waste of your time.

- People in rented accommodation are bad prospects for home improvements as they would not invest their momey in some-one else's property.

- Car finances would be of little use to someone who does not have a driving licence.

- Credit facilities cannot be given to those under 18 years of age.

Ensure that the people your telesales executives are calling are already qualified. If not, either obtain better lists to call from, or ensure that the executives qualify them very early on in the call.

Once the customer is qualified

Once your prospect is qualified, all your telesales executives have to do is to get the potential client or customer to want the product or service. Essentially, this means communicating to them the benefits of having such a service or product in such a way as to make them desire it. The telephone sales executive must be able to convey to the potential client or customer why they should use your product or service, and not a similar product or service which someone else is offering. If your prospect/s are fully qualified, and if your telesales executives have the qualities and skills they need as described earlier in this book, this need not be an onerous task. The only other points to know are these:

1. If the potential customer wants the product or service, they are most of the time waiting for your sales executives to ask for the order.
2. If the telephone sales executive does not ask for the order, they are omitting to ask the most important question of all. Repeatedly, managers and senior sales executives have to remind their sales people that they have to ask for the order. Why is this? Because at the point where you ask for the order, you find out just how effective they have been with the sale. That's the real make-or-break point of the sale. The response is usually an order or a refusal.

Points to remember

- If your potential clients understand the benefits of the service or product/s you are selling, and can afford the product or service, all that is needed to further the sale is good telephone communication skills.

- Four out of five of the people your telesales executives call are waiting for *them* to ask for the order.

- Ask for the business.

An important point:

> Call people at a time that is likely to be suitable for them. Making a call to a busy housewife at nine o'clock in the morning is not necessarily going to get you a good welcome, no matter how much she may like your product. Calling a harassed businessman the moment he walks into his office will not yield the result you want all the time. Be clever. Act smart.

CASE STUDIES

Michael

Michael is determined that all his personnel will understand the products they are selling, inside out, so that there'll never be a question they cannot answer. He knows that if they fully understand the benefits to an individual of the product/services they are selling, they can only do a better job. To this end, he is getting the representatives of the company whose product they are selling to come in and have a full session with his staff to give them the necessary information. He also begins to use better qualified lists than he has been using to date in order to improve his personnel's chances of getting orders. This will cost him more, but he feels the extra is worth it.

Sophie

Sophie has admitted to her manager that there are essential areas of the company's product she actually does not understand much about. He has agreed with her to discuss her queries with one of the technical managers. Sophie feels this will help, as she won't fumble for words when potential clients ask her questions she can't answer. Further, Sophie realises that she has been spending too long on the telephone with people she has failed to properly qualify. Sophie says to her boss: 'It's not that I'm a poor sales-person, just that at times I have totally failed to qualify the prospect in the first place!'

CHECKLIST

1. Bearing in mind the above points, write out your own list of types of customer that it would be wasteful for your team to contact.

2. Review three or four of your past sales attempts which failed. Were the potential clients actually qualified in the first place?

3. How is your current product knowledge? Does it need improving? Are there questions that you dread the potential client asking because you simply do not know the answer? If you find there are, make it your aim this week to get that point cleared up totally.

6

Learning the Mistakes You Can Make as Manager

'If you cannot manage yourself you cannot manage anyone else.'

(Anon.)

DOING THEIR JOB FOR THEM

As discussed earlier in the book, doing the job that your personnel are paid to do is folly. Why should this be?

- It collapses the command and communication lines of any business

- It masks the fact that you are either not training your personnel properly, and/or not hiring effective people, or people who will be effective.

- It prevents the people who should be doing the job from taking their share of responsibility for doing it right.

The answers to this problem are simple:

- Primarily, hire people who fulfil the basic criteria for the position.

- Train them as necessary, both on telesales style as practised by your operation, and in the technical and product information for the service or article you are selling.

- Communicate effectively enough to find out from any slow or ineffective personnel what the difficulty is, and help them to put it right.

Of course, there are some situations whereby you will be doing the work. These are not common situations and should not last for long periods. Examples of such situations could include:

- heavy workload and personnel away sick;
- training ('show me', type of training);
- an important and urgent number of contacts to be called in order to meet an unpredicted demand.

Few other situations would demand your collapse into the telesales executive's chair.

FORGETTING ABOUT PRODUCING

Here are some examples of disorganised managers' habits:

- taking work home;
- arriving late for meetings;
- unpreparedness;
- forgetting important things;
- getting involved in the problems of the staff;
- easily distracted;
- being very busy but producing little;
- arriving late for work;
- getting involved in the emotional content of the office;
- not planning.

This is not a comprehensive list. It could go on and on, but you get the picture. A good manager is organised, and has as their first and primary goal obtaining effective production out of the team.

A manager is not there to be everyone's counsellor, although they will inevitably get involved in listening to staff problems from time to time. Neither is a good and effective manager there to win a popularity contest. Truly effective managers do not have to be popular. If you can achieve true effectiveness as a manager and yet still win the company popularity contest, you are in the minority. There are some stellar examples of both effective and popular managers, but even they have the goals of the company (particularly effective production) first in their thoughts. This does not mean that a good manager has to be hard-hearted, cold and bullying; it means that a good manager manages and gets production as his or her first and primary goal.

Active and reactive tasks

It is important to differentiate between active and reactive tasks. Tasks (things which should be done) normally fall into one of two categories – active tasks and reactive tasks. The active tasks are the things that must be done in order for you to reach the objectives of your job, the production tasks that increase or maintain your quota of products. The reactive tasks are the issues and events which come along and which do not have a direct bearing on producing, but which have to be handled anyway.

Examples of active tasks:

- target setting

- allocation of work

- getting the work done

- creating new contracts and future work

- hiring of new personnel

- training

- motivation.

Examples of reactive tasks:

- de-bugging things which don't work

- bills payment

- sorting out problems due to staff sickness

- personnel problems

- misunderstandings.

Allocate your time and energy in terms of dealing with the active tasks first.

Dealing with active and reactive tasks

Most disorganised managers fall into the trap of only dealing with the reactive tasks and so fail to produce to the required quotas. It is therefore vital to be as ruthless with yourself as is necessary to ensure you allocate time and effort chiefly to active tasks. Active positive tasks must get the lion's share of your attention and are what you should be focused on.

It may be helpful, in a larger operation, to have a deputy or a chief telesales executive to aid you. This person can pick up the reactive tasks, leaving your time and attention free to dedicate to getting on with your primary goal – that of ensuring that quality production is coming from your telesales executives. That way, you can maintain happy customers who will give you repeat orders and business.

Managing a successful telesales team is a living thing. The general tendency has been for this field to attract a more transient employee, the post being regarded as less permanent than other jobs. As a manager, you cannot afford to sit on your laurels for too long. You need to be very proactive.

- If you see things that need to be addressed, you need to act quickly. If someone appears to be a little off on a Monday, you will need to act fast. If you do not act before the Tuesday, you may find that it is already Wednesday, or even Thursday or Friday, and you still have a poorly producing or even non-producing member of staff for whom you are still having to pay out wages – but for no production!

- Have some 'stand-by' staff 'waiting in the wings' to cover losses of personnel. You need a pool of good people whom you can call upon.

WHAT ABOUT NEW BUSINESS?

Do not forget to plan and ensure there are new contracts coming along for the future. Staff hate to be laid off for any period. When staff are laid off, some go straight for another job. If you're lucky, some dedicated few may hang around for a while. Generally, lay-offs are demotivating and embarrassing, to say nothing of bad for cash flow and credibility.

New business has to be created every day. New contracts with existing clients have to be looked after so that they stay with you.

New clients need to be obtained so that when current contracts end, you have more work. Make sure you find out what other contracts your existing clients will require from you when the current one is complete.

The best ways to ensure you get repeat business from your existing clients are:

- Deliver what you promise in the first place.

- Deliver excellent quality products and superlative service.

- Deliver on time, in the right amount.

- Keep in touch with your existing clients – maintain a check to ensure they are pleased with what you are supplying them.

- Deal with any upset or complaint from an existing client immediately.

Know the answers to these questions:
1. How much money do we need to make?
2. What are our expenses?
3. What do we need in sales turnover each year to cover all our expenses and leave us with a profit?
4. What does that mean in weekly sales turnover?
5. What actions must be done as a manager in order to achieve that?

If you do these things regularly, you will be first on the list when it comes to renewing contracts, because you will not have given your existing clients any reason to go looking for anyone else.

CASE STUDY

Michael
Michael has always been a 'hands-on' type of person. He feels it would be out of character not to get involved on a regular basis. He likes to do some of the work himself because it makes him feel 'a part of the team'. Michael is going to need to learn that it is important to maintain his position as manager and change his attitude toward this aspect of management. Michael has already started to work out what 'reactive' tasks he can either delegate or ignore altogether, so that he can focus on increasing his office's

output. He wants to keep the clients he has so is concentrating on ways to improve the quality of product to each of his clients. He recognises that if he can excel with them, they will have no reason to look elsewhere for telesales services.

CHECKLIST

1. Look for the active and reactive tasks that you are doing in your daily work. Are you an active or a reactive manager? How can you rearrange your day in order to focus mainly on production?

2. Examine the work you are producing for your existing clients. Can this be improved in any way to guarantee present and future customer satisfaction How?

3. Always be on the lookout for new business.

7

Learning the Mistakes Your Telesales Executives Can Make

This is not a complete summary of errors and mistakes. Everyone can make a mistake and anyone can perpetuate an error that their peers have been making for a while.

You may have read these common errors before. If so, it certainly will not do any harm to re-read them. If you've not come across them before, do take them 'on board' and watch out for them in your daily activities!

WATCH OUT FOR THESE COMMON ERRORS

Image is important

Of course it is important what you wear and how you look. These have a bearing upon the way you feel, and the way you feel influences the way you communicate and the impression you give to others. Many inexperienced telesales personnel will, however, care more about their personal appearance than the way they appear on the telephone. Telephone image is as important to a telesales executive as personal appearance is to a sales representative.

Your telesales executives can improve their telephone image in some ways:

- Tape their voices. Listening to yourself on tape is a tried and tested method to make sure that you sound the way you want to sound. The tape can also be used to try out different tones of voice, volume, emphasis and diction.

- Have your personnel listen to each other making calls. Listen to them yourself and invite constructive criticism for improvements.

These techniques have been used by singers, speakers, actors and people in the public eye to ensure they sound the way they want to sound. Try it. It works.

Agreeing to send literature – quite unnecessarily

Probably, the most frequent question asked of telesales executives is not 'How would you like me to place the order?' but 'Can you put some literature in the post, and I'll read through it in my own time?' It sounds a fair and reasonable question. After all, don't you like to read things over a cup of coffee and mull it over before you make a decision? Experience has shown, however, that it is not a good idea to routinely send literature for the following reasons:

- Your telesales executive's job is on the telephone, not running around finding literature to put in envelopes.

- It is easy to get the idea that the prospect is interested and is going to pace the floor anxiously waiting for your literature to arrive. (He is not.)

- Your next follow-up call will probably be met with either 'I haven't received it, can you send some more?' or 'I haven't had a chance to read it yet, can you call back in say, three weeks?' So it goes on.

'Please send literature' is not necessarily a sign of interest. Literature will **not** do your telesales executives' job for them. Most often, the literature remains unread until it is either filed away or thrown away.

There are occasions when it may be helpful to send out literature:

- if the request comes later, after you have already made a presentation, then literature should be sent;

- if the customer is genuinely interested to find out more and to maintain his interest until such time as an agreed appointment occurs.

Simply put – just not listening

In order to make an effective sale, appointment or whatever product your telesales executives are aiming for, it is vital that they listen to what the potential customer is telling them. If the telesales executive is not listening, then he or she will not hear the important information from the client that will enable that person to sell effectively to that client. If you have a telesales executive who does not understand this, even after training, then that telesales executive will not be with you for very long.

Listening gives telesales executives most of the information they need to make a successful call.

Failing to see what they're doing

There is a well-known quote, which goes along the lines of – 'doing the same thing over and over, yet expecting, by some strange stroke of luck, a different result'. It may sound absurd, but that is exactly what happens in many telesales offices the world over. The same technique, phraseology, or approach used to poor effect but remaining unchanged. That's why each call should stand alone in the telesales executive's mind as something to be reviewed.

In 'Secrets of the World's Top Sales Performers', (Adams Media Corporation 1990) Sony employees revealed that they get together and discuss their approach and their assumptions. They do not point fingers to place the blame outside or on others. Rather, they decide what caused the poor result and how best to overcome it the next time. It need not take too long. Was that call successful? Why? What made it successful? How can I best repeat the same successful formula? Or why was that call not successful? What did/didn't I do? Was the person at the other end of the line really that bad or could I have dealt with it better? Do not allow your telesales executives to waste such opportunities for learning and improving their skills.

There are a lot of veteran sales people out there who have placed thousands of calls in their lifetime, but have no real experience to speak of. They don't **reflect** on what they have done. It's important to gain experience, but that does not mean having the same experience repeatedly and not learning from it.

Get your telesales executives to reflect on the calls they make. That way they will gain genuine knowledge and improvement. In short, after every call your telesales executives make, have them ask themselves two questions:

1. What did I like about this call?
2. What would I have done differently on this call?

If a feeling of 'there isn't time' or 'I really cannot afford to do this on every single call' persists, just get them to think again. They really cannot afford not to.

Misunderstanding secretaries, telephonists and receptionists

The receptionist, telephonist or the secretary – whichever one it is who answers the telephone, would not be doing their job if they put your telesales executives directly through to their boss without asking you at least a few pertinent questions. Telesales executives must undersatand this. This person is qualifying your personnel to see if they should be put through or just given the cold shoulder, put off or whatever. Getting angry or rude with the secretary will not get calls forwarded. The two rules stated earlier in this book are extremely important here:

- Do not insult the secretary's intelligence with poor telephone skills.

- Make certain you are clear as to what benefits your product may be to the potential client.

To get to your buyers, all you need to do is this: **Help secretaries, telephonists and receptionists (screeners) do their job**. Their job is to protect the buyer's time so that only callers with something of value are allowed to spend time with the boss. Therefore, you need to be sure you have a statement prepared so that you can respond intelligently and clearly when they ask you why you want to speak to their boss. Don't say, 'We sell [x product] and I want to talk to him/her about it.' That normally elicits a response like, 'We're happy with who we're buying from.' Instead, say something like: 'I have some ideas that have helped others in your industry cut down on their maintenance expenses while keeping up a proper programme of repairs. I'd like to ask Mr/Ms Bigg a few questions to see if it would make sense for you to consider them.'

Try it. It works.

Poor (or no) preparation

Decide where you want your telephone call to go. What result are you trying to achieve with that particular person you are calling? In the same way that you wouldn't get out of bed in the morning, get dressed, get in the car and drive off and **then** decide where you are going, so it is important not to make a call until you have prepared some kind of plan for that call.

- Decide where you are with this call and where you want it to go.

- Determine what result you want from the call.

- Firmly establish what it is that you want the potential customer to **do** by the end of the call

Know where you are going with every call and aim to achieve it.

Not asking any or enough questions

- Ask questions.

- Ask more questions

- Listen to the answers.

- You may be uncertain when you initially get through if your product could be of benefit to the potential client. In this case the first thing you will need to do is to qualify the prospect.

The more that you know about an individual, a company and their needs, the easier it is to create a sale.

Misunderstanding objections

More books have been written on this subject ('handling customer objections to buying') than on any other aspect of sales. The truth is this: most customer objections are caused by sales people failing to ask enough questions in the first instance than by any other factor. Effective and pertinent questioning carried on in a professional, amicable and businesslike way will yield more results per call than any amount of 'how to overcome objections' lists, charts or training ever will.

Cunning and clever answers don't get results. When you are faced with a legitimate objection, the best way to tackle it is to ask more questions that are effective. Then you can understand it and possibly deal with it.

- Ask effective questions.

- Listen to the answers.

- If you don't understand the answers, ask more questions.

- Remember that sometimes people don't need what you are selling.

- Don't talk too much. As Albert Einstein said:

> 'If a is success in life, then a equals x plus y plus z. Work is x; y is play; and z is keeping your mouth shut.'

Starting off on the wrong foot

It is well known that within the first minute of meeting someone for the first time impressions are created which immediately set the tone for that relationship. Equally, within the first few seconds of a telephone call, a similar thing happens: either that person is going to be interested in what you have to say or he/she is not. How many times have you picked up the telephone only to be met with: 'Hi, this is Fred Bloggs and I work for Smiths & Sons and we sell blahs. Our company is the biggest in the UK and we recently sent you some literature about our products. I am phoning to tell you more about them.' What would your response be? Most likely your answer would be brief, curt and one of total disinterest. Were you really sitting there just waiting for that call? Almost definitely not.

So what does a professional telesales executive say to get immediate interest? Is there a formula that can be used? Try this:

- Introduce yourself and your organisation. Keep it crisp, clear, concise and amicable.

- Say something that stimulates their interest. This should appeal to their desire to gain or to avoid loss.

- Involve them in a conversation.

For example: 'I'm Ian Smith with Rogers & Co. We specialise in working with the manufacturing industry to keep down their maintenance costs and building work. We have a particularly cost-effective maintenance programme that we think will interest you very much . . .'

Another example: 'This is Beatrice with Kaymex Consulting.

The reason I'm calling is that there is the possibility we might be able to help you cut down on your maintenance budget without cutting back on your maintenance programme. I'd like to ask you a few questions . . .'

The same technique as covered earlier can be applied to this situation. Use colleagues or a tape recorder to find out just how you sound. Would you want to hear more?

Reluctance to get commitment

For a million different reasons, many sales people are reluctant to ask for exactly what it is they want from the potential customer. This usually amounts to:

- failing to ask for the order;

- failing to ask for a start or delivery date;

- failing to ask when, who, where, what and why.

Any sales person can put a tremendous amount of work into a potential sale only to blow it all by their reluctance to get a commitment from the person they have been trying so hard to win over. Sometimes you could feel that the relationship you have built up would suffer if you were to start demanding commitment. Ask yourself this: 'What is the point to all this activity if there is no product at the end of it?'

Create a habit of asking people for the things you need from them. The chances are they will ask you for something in return. What is the problem? In addition, remember this: people can, will and do say 'no'.

- Ask for better tables in restaurants.

- Ask for better service in shops.

- Ask for discounts.

- If you think you deserve it, ask for that raise.

- When you need help, ask for it.

- When things are too noisy, say so. Ask for less noise.

- Overcome any fear you have of asking for the things you need and the commitment you want.

It may be uncomfortable, but it is a very important step on the road to effective professional selling.

Practise the above and you can build a whole new habit of sincerely asking people for commitment.

GETTING OUT FROM UNDER PRESSURE

There is nothing wrong with being under pressure. There is everything wrong in feeling you cannot deal with the amount of pressure you are under. Many excellent books deal with the subject of stress in the workplace or stress in our personal lives and how to deal with it. Therefore, this book touches only lightly upon the subject.

Pressure is what we feel when the tasks we are expected to undertake are too far beyond our resources. While a certain amount of pressure (or stress) can be galvanising and awakening, too much pressure can suppress our desire for and the resources which make success possible.

Here are some ways in which you and your personnel can check the amount of pressure you are under:

- Set realistic targets for your personnel.

- Tell your personnel to let you know if the targets they are set are unrealistic.

- Get enough sleep.

- Eat breakfast.

- Limit the amount of tea, coffee and cigarettes you consume. While they are initially stimulating, they do also tax your body's reasources

- Eat lunch.

- Don't leave disagreements and upsets hanging. Find an appropriate time to resolve issues at work and at home.

- If you don't like the job, find out why and resolve it. Alternatively, find a job that suits you better.

- Don't be afraid to ask for the things you need to make your job run smoother

CASE STUDIES

Michael
Michael fully understands all the information he has learned about telesales mistakes. He should – he's made most of them! 'Learning about your mistakes is not just something you read, then you never make them again,' he says. 'A lot of the errors we make over and over again are the simple, silly ones. Mistakes and misjudgements can be brought about by misunderstandings, and having things in our lives which are not quite right.' In an effort to set up an ongoing awareness of the most common telesales errors, Michael writes out the most common errors in his own words, and even finds a few more which he feels are pertinent. He gets these printed onto posters and placed in strategic places around the operations room of his business. Michael feels this will help everyone to combat them. Michael is also well aware of the pressures people face at work. He resolves to check out his personnel from time to time, and if they appear to be under stress, to do what he can to help them to combat this.

Sophie
Sophie likes the idea of having posters in the office that outline the most common errors. She wants to become as professional as she can. Sophie knows just how reticent she can be, particularly in asking for orders. Although this has not stopped her from achieving a degree of success in telesales, she still wants to improve and 'be the best'.

Roger
Roger has begun to receive a steady flow of appointments for his representative from Michael's company. Pleased with the result, he has no complaint.

CHECKLIST

1. Review the above list of 'common mistakes'. Which of these do you feel you fall down on?

2. What other 'common mistakes' can you see?

3. Work out an approach that is non-confrontational whereby you can address any of the above common mistakes you find with your telesales executives.

4. Pressure – are you under it? Review the areas in your work that you feel need to be addressed. Decide to tackle one of these each week until you feel happier and more comfortable in your work.

8

Calling the Right People

THE TELEPHONE PREFERENCE SCHEME

In 1999, OFTEL (the Office of Telecommunications) appointed the Direct Marketing Association (DMA) to set up and run the new opt-out schemes for unsolicited direct marketing by telephone and fax. The schemes are known as the Telephone Preference Service (TPS) and the Fax Preference Service (FPS). There is no charge for anyone wishing to register with these schemes, both of which give the public the right to protection in their homes from the intrusion of unsolicited faxes and to increased protection from direct marketing telephone calls. Organisations that use the telephone and fax to contact members of the public via unsolicited telephone calls must not contact those who have registered with this opt-out scheme. Telesales companies who breach the regulations can face action by the Data Protection Register, and failure to comply could lead to fines up to £5,000.

For many people unsolicited calls and faxes do constitute an irritating invasion of privacy, and for small firms in particular unwanted faxes can not only be costly, but can also delay important business correspondence.

Direct marketing organisations should contact 01932 414161 for an information pack on the TPS and 0171 766 4422 for an information pack on the FPS. Further information on both these schemes is available on www.oftel.gov.uk.

Telemarketers will be in breach of the regulations if they contact anyone registered with the scheme. There is, however, a 28-day 'period of grace' for telemarketers. This means that if an individual does opt out they may still receive calls for up to 28 days from the period of registering. This is to allow telemarketers time to update their lists etc. Thus companies involved in direct marketing must refresh their list of people who may not be contacted not less than every 28 days.

When making a direct marketing call, you are under an obligation to provide the person/s you are calling with certain information to enable them to identify and where necessary to contact you. The regulations require the caller to identify the company or organisation making the call and, when requested, to provide either a contact address or a freephone telephone number on which your organisation can be contacted.

There are now many marketing companies actively involved with both the TPS and FPS. Many of the more amateur companies continue to call potential customers directly from telephone directories and other badly vetted sources. Not only can this lead to problems with the TPS, but can be a huge waste of time and money through poor customer qualification.

Lists that have not been TPS checked can place yourselves and your company in a troublesome situation. Fully TPS and FPS qualified lists are readily available from reputable suppliers. They cost more of course, but there are no court costs involved!

Smaller marketing companies who carry out a far lower rate of telemarketing will probably not use the TPS lists, and because of the lower number of calls involved stand a far greater chance of 'getting away with it'. The higher your call rate, the larger your operation, the greater the possibility one of your telemarketers is going to find themselves calling someone who has opted out. So you run a higher risk of TPS contravention the bigger your operation is. Five hundred calls per day per telemarketer times the number of telemarketers times the number of days each works adds up to the risk you run if you are not using the Telephone Preference Scheme. The bigger your operation, the more you need to be aware of the Telephone Preference Scheme and act in accordance with it.

MAKING AND CHANGING APPOINTMENTS –
WHAT TO SAY

Any appointment has to fulfil two basic criteria:

- It has to be convenient to the customer.

- It has to be convenient to the company's representative.

If your telesales executives insist upon making an appointment that is not truly convenient to the customer, things start to go wrong. You run risks. The risks are that the customer will be either out or unavailable when the representative calls, or the customer will call back before the appointment's date and time and cancel. Neither of these is good for business.

The appointment that your telesales executive makes can be at a time when the sales representative would not normally schedule a visit. You therefore run the risk of the sales representative contacting the client directly to change the time or date of the appointment. Alternatively, the sales representative may ask you to change the time of the appointment. Neither of these is particularly acceptable because:

- they both involve 'negative' contact with the customer;

- they make your business look unprofessional;

- they provide an opportunity for the potential customer to cancel the appointment altogether. (A well qualified prospect who has been 'sold' an appointment correctly should not be looking for ways to back out – but that does not mean to say that you should offer an opportunity for him or her to do so.)

Therefore, where making appointments is a part of their brief, it is very important that telesales executives are both succinct and clear in the manner in which they make appointments.

Making an appointment

- Offer a date which you know is convenient to the sales representative.

- Offer a time which you know is convenient to the sales representative.

- Gain the customer's agreement on both the date and time, reading it back to them for confirmation.

- (Make certain that the customer understands how long the Sales Representative will be with them.)

Changing an appointment

Sometimes, there is no alternative but to change an appointment. When it is necessary to do so, prepare first. Ensure that you have to hand at least two dates and times (which you know are 100 per cent convenient for the sales representative). Then, follow the steps above to gain a new appointment with the client. Courtesy alone dictates that an apology should be given. However, it is important to keep the telephone call both brief and formal so as not to allow any negativity or tendency to cancel on the part of the customer.

HAVING THE RIGHT ATTITUDE

> What is the correct attitude for anyone working within the telesales industry? Is telesales really 'just a numbers game'? Or is it a profession?

If telesales were just a numbers game (which some people consider the case), then this would be the philosophy:

> It really does not matter whom you hire or call. Rent a room, put some telephones in, and hire anyone, as long as they're cheap. Tell them, 'Your target is x, make the calls, get the sales, make your target or you're out by the end of the month.' Have them use telephone directories at the rate of 100 calls per hour. It's a numbers game, the more calls they make, the more sales they get.

However, telesales is a professional activity engaged in by professional people. Therefore, the right attitude and the right philosophy is that professional people, properly trained, making contact with properly qualified prospects using appropriate skills and equipment, correctly managed, will succeed and win both commercially and personally.

CASE STUDIES

Michael

Michael knows very well that many consider telesales to be purely a numbers game. He resolves to ensure that all his personnel think of themselves as professionals. He calls in the sales representatives for a meeting with his telesales executives. As a team, they can then discuss the correct scheduling of appointments. In addition, they can clarify any issues the sales representatives may have about this.

Sophie

Sophie always makes the point of speaking to 'her' sales representative on a daily basis and because of this they have a good
working relationship. If for any reason one of her appointments
has to be rescheduled, she discusses her approach with him to
adopt the correct strategy.

Roger

Roger has supplied Michael with a list of companies and people
who either live or run businesses in the local area and for whom
he has carried out work. He also includes those 'contacts' that he
likes to speak to personally. He ensures that the information he
passes on includes people with whom he does **not** wish to do
business, so that Michael's' company does not contact them. Some
of these people are reputed 'bad risks' and others he knows to be
already using alternative sources with which they are content, and
whose prices he knows he cannot 'beat' at this time.

CHECKLIST

1. How have you handled the remaking of appointments in the
   past? Was this successful?

2. Why are customers more likely to cancel an appointment if it is
   necessary to call them to change it? What other options can
   you think of?

3. How do you see yourself as a telesales manager? Are you a
   'numbers game' person? On the other hand, do you consider it
   a profession? Work out for yourself the long-term result of
   each of the above philosophies.

9

More on Setting Up and Running Your Own Telesales Department

GETTING IN ALL THE BASICS

The environment in which telesales executives work has an important impact upon the quality of their work. A poor environment is not conducive to good quality production. Poor equipment will have a similar effect. This is covered fully in the next chapter.

Chairs, seating and other equipment all have an effect upon the way a telesales executive feels. Often, in office and other work environments with poor atmosphere and equipment, there is a high turnover of staff. The standards that are set in the office or workplace reflect the ethos and professionalism of the company and its management, and the manner in which the business is run. If a company will not invest in good equipment and an acceptable environment for its personnel, then it may be that it is not worth working for that comapny.

The impression that any outbound telesales company needs to create is one of professionalism, upmarket values, smartness, accuracy and competence. The more this is present in the workplace, the easier it communicates to the customer. Television advertising often features outbound call centres as the background to an actor talking about a product and suggesting that we 'call now'. This type of effect is normally created within a TV studio, of course, but the image is right.

Again, every industry that requires a level of customer contact has to employ people who are appropriate for that job. As you would not employ a car mechanic to do the job of a sales respresentative, so you need to have people with the right attributes and skills to become successful telesales executives and convey the right image to your clients.

DOING IT HEALTHILY AND SAFELY

All businesses within the UK are subject to certain rules and regulations concerning health and safety. You can find information relating to health and safety measures for business in various places, such as:

- public libraries;
- your nearest Health and Safety Executive office;
- small business centres;
- there will be a local Health and Safety Office listed in your telephone book;
- there are numerous leaflets and other material, books, etc published in order to make known the rules and regulations that govern your business.

Whether you will be running your own business from its own premises or acting as manager for a department within a company, it is important that you are aware of the health and safety issues for your premises. These will cover such things as:

- fire escapes and fire extinguishers;
- fire alarms;
- electrical safety;
- emergency contingencies (such as fire escape plans, what to do in the event of an emergency, etc.);
- general 'dos and don'ts' for different types of working environment.

In larger companies a health and safety officer is normally appointed whose job it is to know the regulations applicable to his company. They would also be the person to whom any staff would go in order to find out information about health and safety issues. In a small company, that person is normally the manager or a named executive.

Information on health and safety

Although often considered a boring an uninteresting side of business, health and safety is both an interesting and essential aspect of any business. There is a wide range of leaflets available from the H&SE covering every aspect of safe conduct and wise health procedures in the workplace. You can get hold of literature that advises on:

- risk assessment (the likelihood of problems balanced against the need to get something done);
- planning office layout;
- temperature settings (both for comfort and safety);
- smoking;
- workstations;
- maximising natural resources (such as light);
- ergonomics (correct seating and standing posture, etc.);
- types of equipment to use;
- noise in the workplace;
- protective measures.

Find out your nearest H&SE office and talk to them.

GETTING THE BUSINESS

Obtaining new business and maintaining your current levels of business are going to be an extremely important facet of your operation. Without clients to work for, nothing will happen.

It is important, as discussed earlier in this book, to pitch your operation so that you are working with clients who are the 'right size' for the business you are or you want to be – match yourselves to your client.

- If you are going to be a one-man band, working with one telephone line, you should not be targeting multinational companies for business. The number of calls they will expect you to make in a week will far exceed your resources.

- If you have a large team of people, you should not be targeting a one-man business. You can afford to deal with the larger clients.

- Match your business to the business with which you want to do business.

Much business-to-business contact is now carried on via e-mail and the Internet as well as by post, telephone and fax. As the world of telephone sales is expanding, so is the amount of business done through the Internet and e-mail (e-commerce). Many companies have their own website that details their services, products and gives important information about the company. Nearly all websites will allow direct contact through e-mail to the correct person within the company you may need to approach. E-commerce is the way of the future.

Your potential customers will differ depending on who you decide to work for. Some telesales companies now decide to stay out of the domestic market because of the poor image that has been generated in this area by unprofessional methods. So there are telesales companies that only work business to business. The personnel in these companies will therefore work Monday to Friday business hours. Other companies that do call residential properties employ their staff on hours appropriate to getting though when people are at home. Therefore, you will need to take the hours your team can and will work into account when determining who your clients are going to be.

Websites
Some telesales companies have their own website which acts as a permanent information point about the company and allows direct contact via e-mail from potential clients too. Setting up your own website will involve you in extra cost of course. The design of the site and the ongoing cost of making it accessible to your public will have to be taken into consideration when planning your marketing budget. It should be considered as an option, if only because so many people are now turning to the Internet to supply their business needs.

How do I attract new business?
Here are some options:

- Radio advertisements.

- Television advertisements.

- Local press.

- National press is another excellent way to attract business.

- Invite along local companies to look at your premises and the way you work.

What is the best way to get business?

Well, you have a telesales business to hand, why not use it to get your own business?

Initially you need a thoroughly worked out marketing strategy:

- What type of customers do you want?

- Where do you want to go with the strategy?

- Find out if customers have a high opinion of the brand and product.

- Ensure that your company will be able to live up to any promises it makes.

- Deliver the right product to the right place at the right time in the right quantity.

- Thoroughly read and understand any terms and conditions on every contract that you sign. If it isn't clear, get it clarified – before you sign.

- Deal with customer complaints by acknowledging mistakes and rectifying errors immediately.

- Make certain that both you and your telesales executives are knowledgeable about the product or service you are selling.

- Check that your customer is happy with the way in which you and your team are performing.

- Keep a measure of the percentage of your total calls which turn into sales.

- Analyse the results of your top performers.

- Don't feel you have to solve all the problems.

- When the client comes to you, agree sales targets (1,000 sales per year, for example).

- Do what we say we're going to do.

Some companies will pay you by results. Others will pay by the hour/day/week/month. When being paid by commission, you have to be very confident that you can sell the product concerned.

A manager's role is different from that of the telesales executive. Planning, organising and pragmatism are more the manager's hallmarks than those of the telesales executive. A good telesales manager should strive to get things done properly, in a pragmatic and organised manner. The planning and control of a successful telesales team is vitally important.

CASE STUDIES

Michael
Michael has arranged for the local fire brigade to come along and check that his offices meet the required standards. He has also reviewed the strategy he worked out earlier to confirm that he has the correct clientele and that his products are 'rolling off the line', as they should.

Roger
Roger has given Michael a letter stating just how pleased he is with the service he receives from Michael's company. This will inevitably gain him some form of discount in the future, while being another promotional feather in Michael's cap.

CHECKLIST

1. What do I need to set up the office?

- desks

- chairs

- tables

- telephones

- heating

- ventilation
- computers
- other telephone equipment
- footrests
- sales personnel
- training facilities
- paperwork (contracts, etc.)
- schedules for personnel

2. Is the office environment conducive in terms of decor/posters/atmosphere?

- logs for personnel
- toilet facilities
- tea/coffee facilities
- appropriate directories, etc.
- writing equipment
- receptionist.

3. Check around the office. What health and safety improvements need to be made? Are there sufficient fire extinguishers? Is access to the fire exits clear and open?

10

Choosing the Right Equipment

HEADSETS AND TELEPHONES

The equipment your personnel use is **important**. Don't let others tell you any different. Like the sales representative who looks forward to his or her new car every two years, so the telesales executive deserves to enjoy good equipment. Good, practical equipment does make a difference. The sales representative drives the car every day; it's a tool of the profession. The staff work area, tools and equipment, like the sales rep's car, say something about them and the way in which they do their job.

Comfort and professionalism
As the major tool of this trade is the telephone, it is important to give serious thought to comfort, ease of use, practicality and, or course, cost. Let us look at some available options to help you become more comfortable, more professional, and more under control.

Headsets

Headsets (a telephone mouthpiece and earpiece which clip over the head) are available in a range of styles and prices. The price depends upon the degree of sophistication and the quality of the headset. At the time of writing, headsets range in price from £30 up to £250.

Some advantages of using a headset are:

- Hands are free to write, use a keyboard or turn pages.

- Individuals may feel they can have a more natural conversation.

- The headset often helps personnel to cope with a noisy environment.

- The possibility of repetitive strain injury is reduced.

- Headsets often look and feel more 'professional'. This could improve the performance of personnel.

Quick release
Some headsets have a 'quick release' facility, enabling them to be disconnected from the telephone line in order to leave the desk, and simply plugged back in again when reseating. This is advantageous if your personnel need to move around a lot within the work area. Modern headsets are lightweight, easy to wear and remarkably efficient.

Comfort
A headset may not be appropriate for the casual telephone user, and there are those who 'just feel right' holding the telephone receiver when making a call. However, a headset may be ideal for your personnel. Telecommunications companies have a range of headsets that are available to purchase over the counter or to order. BT has an excellent range in their shops. If those you order turn out to be inappropriate, you can simply return them or change them for an alternative style or model.

Telephones
Many modern telephones are equipped with an extra socket for a headset. These allow the headset and handset to be used simultaneously as a training aid. You can monitor the staff member's handling of the telephone call. If the telephone has a 'secrecy' button, you can also give on-line coaching (see below).

Handset adapters
Some telephone handsets will allow an adapter to be clipped on which allows the handset to be held comfortably between the shoulder and neck. These are a good alternative to headsets, but may give insufficient freedom of movement.

Features to look for
It is suggested that you consider one or more of these features when deciding upon a telephone for telesales use:

- Clearly visible and easy-to-press buttons – numbers can be tapped out easily and clearly – why waste valuable time?

- Last number redial facility – this is a very useful function for those customers who are engaged or who want to be called back in a few minutes. If someone forgets to check something – just press the button and they are back in touch.

- Headset socket – as detailed above, there are many advantages to a headset.

- Lightweight handset – heavy handsets may become un-comfortable with prolonged use

- Hands-free facility – if the telephone user does not have a headset, a hands-free facility on the telephone will make some tasks easier, particularly if it is necessary to shuffle papers or write a lot.

Some other useful features

- A volume control – some people speak very quietly, but asking the person at the other end of the telephone to 'speak up' is not always appropriate. With a volume control, this difficulty can be surmounted.

- Dialler display – this shows the number being called.

- A longer, flexible lead between handset and main unit – short and rigid handset leads inhibit easy movement.

- A 'secrecy' button – it may be necessary to check something with a colleague, and a secrecy button means this can be done without the person at the other end of the line overhearing. It also means that, as a manager, you can give coaching while your staff are actually on the telephone.

Not all of these features may be required for good telephone work. Different equipment suits different people. It is as well to be aware of the many options available, however.

Try these tips

- Observe your department when it's busy. Do any personnel appear uncomfortable with the telephones you have? Try to see why.

- Purchase a headset for your department. Let different members of staff use it. See what they think of it. Do they find it comfortable? Does it increase their activity?

- Buy a telephone with the above features. Let some of your personnel try it out. Use it yourself. Does it make a difference to the way you work?

- If headsets prove popular with your staff, would it be attractive to offer them as incentives for high achievers?

PROJECT-TRACKING SOFTWARE AND COMPUTERS

Some areas of the telesales industry require repeated contact to a wide base of people in order to bring about a sale. In these fields, it is vital to be able to keep track of large quantities of information and the numerous telephone calls made. This is where project-tracking software applies.

Using project-tracking software

Project tracking software is often found within the construction industry, where major building projects can involve ten to twenty different companies and hundreds of people. Records of names, dates and progress have to be kept as it becomes vital to know who is involved in the project, who needs to be spoken to and what their telephone, fax, mobile and e-mail details are. Keeping to strict deadlines with calls is vital using such a system. There may be only one day in a month when you will be able to speak to key people, and these important calls cannot be missed. Such telephone sales activity is known as 'project tracking' or 'project coordination' and requires extensive telephone work to a wide range of people. These include architects, project engineers, designers, planners, surveyors and estimators.

Managers

Managers find this type of software extremely useful. It allows them to see exactly what calls have been made, to whom and by whom. Good project-tracking software will also allow a manager to key in a sales person's name and find out how their call rate compares to others, what effect the calls are having upon overall sales, and any of a wide permutation of factors which allows them to be fully informed.

Coordinating projects

Project coordinators and managers will normally utilise specially designed computer software programs in order to keep accurate records. These records cover progress made, who has been contacted and by whom, the names of important figures who make decisions, etc. The sales basics are the same, but the use of the computer and software program adds an additional element.

The project coordinator will have the PC available, entering in important dates and information on a daily basis. Software for project tracking will also allow the entry of other information such as what was discussed, important dates, personal views and when the next telephone call should be. It also allows cross-referencing to other projects. On an appropriate day in the future, the computer will notify the project coordinator that a return telephone call is due. Utilising such a system, it should be possible to keep track of a very large number of different projects. The software does the work, but the scheduled telephone work still has to be done, and all new information has to be entered into the system.

Many companies also use this system as an aid to follow up literature on specific dates, say eight to ten days after it has been sent. Managers, as detailed above, find it an invaluable tool both for day-to-day management and for use in predicting sales forecasts.

Advantages of project-tracking systems

- Ease of tracking many different contacts in a wide base of businesses.

- One person is able to keep track of and coordinate complex activity.

- Sales can be monitored and managed by the sales person and executives.

- Record keeping is precise and records are available.

- Vast amounts of information, easily accessible, can be called upon to focus sales activity.

- Set up and running properly, executives can keep a 'finger on the pulse' of a wide range of projects, sales activity and the effectiveness of sales campaigns.

Disadvantages of project-tracking systems

- Problems can arise if the information is not entered into the system or entered in incorrectly.

- When the system goes down, so does a high percentage of sales activity.

- Such systems cost money, in capital outlay, in training and maintenance.

OTHER USEFUL TOOLS

There are many other tools which may help to make telephone sales life more comfortable, more ordered and more manageable. While some of these may not be relevant to your particular needs, they are all useful tools.

Residential and business telephone directories on CD

Telephone directories are now available on CD to save time and money. If your company utilises computer systems as sales tools, this simple and versatile extra can be invaluable. With millions of names, addresses and telephone numbers of potential residential and business customers, it is something worth thinking about. Of course, this depends upon the size and scope of your business calling.

Increasing your comfort with office equipment

- The use of footrests is becoming increasingly common in the workplace. They are available in a range of heights, styles and materials. A footrest can make all the difference to the level of personnel comfort and can therefore add to sales activity.

- Employ proper seating. There is no end of office seating stores. Good seating costs little and can make a tremendous difference to the quality of work. Good seating means that personnel are more comfortable, more relaxed and more in control.

- Sitting at a desk or work surface of the correct height with enough room to write with ease can make a difference to the productivity of staff.

- Acoustic dividers between desks can create a calmer work environment where staff can be more relaxed and feel more able to communicate one to one with their clients. They also allow you to work with staff on a one-to-one basis for training purposes.

Remember that it is important to have the right equipment for the job. Good equipment costs money of course, but properly equipped personnel can also carry out a far more effective job.

CASE STUDIES

Michael
Michael is trying the various options. He has separated his eight personnel into two groups of four, and four of these are trying out headsets for one week. After this trial, Michael is going to upgrade the telephones he uses for his other four telesales executives and see if they like the extra facilities. After this, he can review the results and determine if it will be worth purchasing better telephones and headsets for his team.

Sophie
Sophie isn't sure. She likes all these new ideas, but still feels that successful telesales is somehow dependent upon the ability to be forceful and pushy. She feels that smart equipment is good, but it's what she says on the telephone that is most important. Of course, Sophie is quite correct. After a discussion Sophie came around to the fact that, although it is most important to communicate and listen correctly on the telephone, it is also important to be comfortable and to be able to control the equipment, papers and other 'tools of the trade'. Sophie is going to try using a headset to see if it will assist her with the administrative side of the job. In addition, she feels that it would look and feel very professional to wear a headset, 'once I've got used to the idea of having my hands free'.

Roger
Roger is certain. After visiting Michael's office, he likes the look and feel of some of the new equipment and so is obtaining some for his receptionist. Roger is impressed with the standard of

Michael's office equipment and how professional it looks. This serves to increase his confidence in the company.

CHECKLIST

There are many tools available to make your telephone sales work easier and more professional.

- appropriate telephone/s
- headsets
- desks and seating
- other telephone facilities
- computers
- software programs.

11

Telesales from Home

AN OVERVIEW

'Outsourcing' is now a common term meaning that work is carried on outside the main company premises. This has come of age now that computers, faxes and e-mail are readily avilable to all. Home-based telesales executives are common now and there are no reasons why it cannot be as effective to work from home as it is to work from an office provided that simple rules are followed. 'Teleworking' is not only about the physical workplace; some of the major issues surrounding teleworking are psychological; for example, factors such as isolation and the ability to work with limited social contact are important.

Teleworking from home can be fun and exciting, and means that many excellent teleworkers can earn good money while doing a professional job **and** look after children when they arrive home from school. However, working from home makes special demands on people and some will be unable to adapt. The UK's Department of Employment suggests that the following are important qualities for home teleworkers:

- maturity
- trustworthiness
- self-sufficiency
- self discipline
- good time management skills
- good communication skills.

Obviously, it is important to look for these qualities when selecting personnel if you are seriously considering having some or all of your teleworkers working from home. It is also important for those who think they may be good at teleworking from home to check themselves against those points. Certain organisations use psychological tests or trained counsellors to help the individual employee work out whether they are compatible with the demands of teleworking.

Potential problems should be highlighted and the organisation's ground rules must be made clear. It is important to make potential staff aware they will not be able to look after their children or pets or perform domestic tasks when they should be working. It should be emphasised that time constraints will be the same as they are in any office.

DOING IT EVERY DAY – WHY BECOME EXHAUSTED?

For the individual, 'freelance' telesales executive working from home, as with any work environment, there are potential distractions, but there are even more so when from home. Some of these may be:

- an over-relaxing environment;
- no one to watch over you;
- daytime TV;
- proximity to coffee, tea, food and a whole host of other potential distractions.

Basic rules for homeworkers

However, if a few simple rules are followed, there is no reason why a determined home-based teleworker cannot produce good results. The key to productivity when working on the telephone from home is to **be your own good manager**.

1. Set yourself targets. Make them do-able, but not too easy. Keep a record of your number of calls, response and success rates from previous days and weeks and aim to better it every day. If you do this, you will also be able to note your weak points and therefore understand what areas need improvement (closing, getting through to the key person, record-keeping, etc.).
2. Have an area dedicated to your work and only to your work. Do not allow other household matters to clutter it (bills, letters to write, etc.).

3. Before you begin work each day, ensure that there are no interruptions likely to occur. Ensure the dog is fed and watered, the cats are in/out, the children, if there are any, know that you are now working, etc.
4. While a friendly telephone call can be a welcome distraction, discipline yourself to tell personal telephone callers that you are working now, and would they please call you later (or you'll call them back when you finish work).
5. Keep in touch with your office or line manager once daily, if you have one.
6. Regard yourself as a professional who works from home.
7. Any telesales executive should **take regular short breaks away from the telephone**. A few minutes in every 45 minutes or so will make all the difference (see below).

Forget the uninterested

From time to time, you will find that there are certain people you are trying to contact who repeatedly turn up on every list you have to call back. When this becomes a chore, there is a very simple solution: remove them from the list. You've left messages, they don't call back. Whenever you do call, they are 'in a meeting', 'out of the office', 'busy at the moment'. Get the message? Your call is not wanted. Just strike them off. You will find this both a refreshing way to deal with those names that come up all the time, and it keeps you firmly in the driving seat. There are millions and millions of householders out there, and hundreds of thousands of companies. You really do not need to keep plugging the same ones. Unless, of course, there's something truly exceptional about that particular name. That is doubtful.

Take a break!

Take regular breaks away from the telephone and your work area. Even if it means just walking round the garden or the house. Every 45 minutes to an hour, get up and transfer your attention to something (a) at a different focus, (b) on a different subject, (c) that will utilise your legs. You'll get far less weary this way and come back feeling refreshed. If a telephone call has left you feeling low, hopeless or angry, get away from your workstation and do something else for five minutes. Come back and carry on only when you're feeling ready.

DEALING WITH RECORDS AND PAPERS

Records are important. You need to know what you have done. Don't rely on a philosophy of 'I'll remember that' or 'I'll make a note of that later'. Such a system has proved to be better off with the dinosaurs (and look what happened to them). Whether or not you have an excellent memory – commit it to paper, notebook, diary, disc, or whatever. Then you can recall it with no problem.

1. Make notes in a neat and orderly way as you progress through your calls.
2. Keep all papers neat and tidy.

Have some type of form that prompts you through the details you have to make note of. Include such things as:

- Did you get to speak to the essential person?

- Was the call successful?

- Do you need to call back?

- When do you need to call?

The items you will need to carry on even the most basic form of telesales from home are:

- paper, pens;

- product information;

- a good telephone (see Chapter 8);

- a quiet, separate space;

- a desk or table;

- details of who is to be called (whether this is a telephone book or something more specific and comprehensive).

Papers multiply by themselves, it seems. Keep all papers neatly, ideally in a ring binder. You never know when you are going to need to refer to some product literature or a past record, so have them arranged in a folder, binder or a type of filing system which is very easily accessible and which suits you.

Invest in a computer

If you can, invest in a computer and software which does away with the need for paperwork. Of course, there will still be some paperwork, but storing information on a PC is the preferred option. In addition to this, back up files regularly. Most PCs these days, even at the lower end of the market, come with some form of organisational software. If you can obtain a reasonably priced PC, and learn to use the software, you can upgrade your home-based operations considerably. You may even then be able to carry out work for several different companies during your working week. As nearly all PCs today also come with Internet software, you will also have the facility to send and receive e-mail, which can be a great help where written information and/or confirmations are requested.

CASE STUDY

Chas

Chas was an excellent communicator and had sales experience. He got a job working from home as a teleseller with an insurance company, making appointments for the sales representative. After four days, Chas was unable to make any appointments, so asked his manager for advice. Instead of getting help and advice, Chas's manager sacked him, gave him a cheque for money owed, collected the telephone directories he'd given, and that was that. Chas didn't get involved in home telesales again.

- The manager didn't make certain that Chas knew the job at all.
- Chas failed to understand that he was expected to produce in good quantity from day one.
- There was no training, no support.

The moral is that, if you're doing telesales from home – be careful. Not everyone who offers you work is going to be a good employer. Get a contract and read it before you sign it. You could end up seriously out of pocket, especially if you've used your own telephone line but have not been successful in gaining sales or appointments.

CHECKLIST

1. Have you considered working from home in telesales? Go through the above points to make certain that you will be able to fulfil the basic criteria.

2. Do you have home teleworkers? If so, how do they measure up in terms of the above as regards their production?

3. What are the advantages/disadvantages from your point of view of having home teleworkers?

12

Goals, Motivation and Staying the Course

REVIEWING YOUR GOALS

Having goals and working toward them is, essentially, what gets us out of bed in the morning. It is vitally important to have objectives and goals.

Picture yourself as an explorer. Far away, you can see a high plateau that you want to reach. Between you and the plateau are valleys, deserts, forests and deep mists. In your progress towards the plateau, it would disappear from sight from time to time as you travel through the forests, valleys and mists. The plateau will always be there, although it will be out of view a lot of the time. However, you will always remember to look for it.

Even as a football player, you would have a goal. You may not have control of the ball for much of the time, and you will become involved in tackles and long tactical manoeuvres of the ball, but you will never forget that to score a goal is your overall objective. Your personal and business goals are just the same. They may disappear from view from time to time because of the various problems and activities you become involved in, but you should always remember to keep your goals in mind and make sure you are heading in their direction.

Keep your objectives clear

As a manager or a telesales executive, make sure that your goals and objectives are clear, that you always keep them in mind and that you ensure you are working towards them. The more your own goals and objectives line up with the goals and ideals of your job, the greater your successes will be.

Everything in the effective telesales manager's operations room should be deliberately designed to promote production and be as inspirational and as upmarket as the budget will allow. Posters (with an inspirational message) add to the atmosphere.

Key managerial traits

There are of course, important traits that any manager needs to possess in order to be a good and effective manager and these are outlined elsewhere in this book. However, some obvious denominators common to all good executives are as follows:

- A leader must be competent. Competence is a test that your personnel will expect you to meet. Incompetent managers and leaders usually hold power for only a very short period before they are removed from office. Competence is being able to do the things you are supposed to be able to do, with minimum effort and with maximum result. The way in which people would normally become competent is by excellent training and positive experience.

- A leader must be able to communicate. Any manager has to be able to communicate with his personnel, the public and his own seniors. Therefore, they must have communications skills that will allow them to get the message across to a variety of different people in a medley of different situations. Skills in communicating must include both soft (sympathetic, empathetic, compassionate) communications skills and hard (demands, orders, commands and instructions) communications skills. Any manager will be called upon to take disciplinary action from time to time so they must be able to communicate their feelings and thoughts about undesirable behaviour and activity effectively. Conversely, a manager will also have to use softer approaches to more delicate situations where calmness and a thoughtful manner are more appropriate.

- A manager must have an affinity for the area they are responsible for, and be able to relate to it realistically. Furthermore, they must be able to relate very well to the problems and difficulties being experienced by the people doing work in that area. Managers who are 'out of touch' also do not last long as managers in today's business climate.

Your own plans

It would be pointless expecting other people to meet targets and have goals and expectations of themselves if you didn't have the same ideals for yourself. Therefore, make certain that you know exactly where you want to go as a telesales manager and what it is that you are out to achieve. Have your plans written up so that you can refer back to them and work towards them.

Many companies today have their senior executives' own criteria for success printed out and on display in order to increase understanding with their workforce. If you do this, it can bring about a greater understanding with your personnel of exactly what it is you are trying to achieve. You may even receive input back from your personnel on ways to improve upon it!

HOLDING SALES MEETINGS

Often considered the bane of sales personnel, sales meetings **should** be an invaluable tool – invaluable not only for building and maintaining team spirit, but to get vital information across (in both directions) and to exchange ideas and experiences.

Meetings with your personnel are invaluable for building and maintaining team spirit, celebrating success, informing the team of new plans and a whole host of other information. The most effective meetings are those which allow plenty of time and opportunity for feedback.

Of course, the mood of your meetings will be influenced by the latest sales figures, because that is what you are all working for. But try not to let such meetings become punitive or an occasion for a wholesale 'telling off' of your personnel. Constructive criticism coupled with objective analysis of any difficulties can be motivating and also stimulate input from the team to help solve any difficulties. Always make your team feel that it is a winning and successful team, even though it may have setbacks.

There is no reason why you should not invite some of your clients along to your sales meetings, so that they can 'get the feel' of the team who will be working to sell their products for them. This is also an excellent way in which to deal with any real problems your team may be facing with selling the client's product or service.

Customers are usually very happy to assist you to sell their products, and may come up with ideas and solutions which you may not have thought of.

PAYING COMMISSION AND BONUSES

There are very important rules about paying commission and bonuses. Exactly the same rules apply to wages:

- pay wages on time and ensure the correct amount is paid to the correct person;
- pay commissions when they are due, exactly as agreed;
- pay bonuses when you agree to pay them to those who have earned them.

Whatever the pay structure that is pertinent to your operation, ensure that your personnel understand it thoroughly. Always make sure it is published and every employee has a copy. More disagreements and upsets are caused over discrepancies between what an employee thinks they should have been paid and what they actually are paid than anything else. This does not necessarily mean that you have to pay everyone the same, of course. Just make sure that employees understand exactly what their individual pay agreement is, put it in writing and have them sign a copy.

Some successful telesales companies pay commission monthly, others weekly. It all depends on the type of products your telesales executives are dealing with and the financial arrangements you have worked out with your clients.

While you may be lucky enough to have people working for you simply because they like the job, it is money in the form of basic salary, commission and bonuses which will motivate most of your personnel. As money is such an important motivator, it is important to keep the flow of money on time, accurate and as agreed.

CASE STUDIES

Michael

Michael has issued contracts and agreements to each of his personnel. These accurately reflect the pay and commission structure that he has agreed individually with each member of staff. He gets each of his personnel to sign a copy, and now has a sound basis on which to resolve any disagreements over money. He is also holding weekly sales meetings where any successes and problems are fully discussed with his personnel. Once a month he invites along a representative from one of the companies for whom he is working. His personnel can then build up a good working relationship with these companies.

Sophie
Sophie has asked her manager to put in writing what has already been agreed with regard to her pay and commission. She feels this will help resolve any potential future disagreements.

CHECKLIST

1. Write down your goal as manager. Is it something worth achieving?

2. What do you think would be a basic format for a weekly staff meeting?

3. Do you think that pay and commission structures should always be agreed in writing? Why is this?

13

Telesales Questions and Answers

WHY DO SO MANY PEOPLE HAVE A LOW OPINION OF TELESALES ACTIVITY?

In the residential sector, it is particularly true that many people dislike and distrust telesales calls. The essential reasons for this bad feeling are:

- telesales personnel calling at times which are inconvenient for the client;

- telesales personnel attempting to sell goods or services which are inappropriate;

- telesales personnel not listening.

You need to make effective calls. In order to make an effective call, telesales personnel must ensure the potential client is qualified (has a need or desire for and the ability to pay for the product or service). It is also important that it is a convenient moment for them to take the call. Telesales activity is a friendly activity intended to foster good sales and goodwill, so it is important to behave in a friendly, responsible and professional manner toward the people you are calling.

'Telesales' has become synonymous with 'annoying' for many people. As professionals, we must work towards changing this. It is important, however, to remember that no one can please everybody. If you feel that you have acted in a friendly and professional manner but you still end up with a negative response, don't lose too much sleep over it!

WHAT IS THE MOST EFFECTIVE THING I CAN DO FOR SUCCESS IN TELESALES?

As a manager there are three key activities in which you need to be competent and active:

- Gain and use a very full understanding of exactly what it is that your activity should be producing. Make sure all your actions count toward this.

- Recruit only competent personnel (as outlined elsewhere in this book) and ensure they are trained fully in the products or services you are selling.

- Establish a culture of professionalism within your team – professional listening, professional communication, professional sales technique.

As a telesales executive, persistence and competence are keywords to your success. If you bear in mind the following, you will succeed where others do not:

- Qualify your prospects. Don't waste your time and effort calling people who will not need, want or be able to afford the products or services you have to offer.

- Understand fully all aspects of the product or service you have to offer. If you cannot answer a potential customer's question on one occasion, make sure you can the next time. There is no substitute for a full understanding of the benefits of your product or service to the customer.

- Listen to what the person at the other end of the line is saying to you. If you don't understand their reasoning, ask questions.

- Believe and have confidence in the product or service that you are selling. If you understand it, but still don't have confidence in it, find something else to sell!

I HAVE A HIGH TURNOVER OF PERSONNEL IN MY TELESALES DEPARTMENT. WHAT CAN I DO ABOUT THIS?

Good sales people do tend to move around. Often this is due to a better remuneration package being offered to them. If you want to keep your good sales people:

- provide excellent working conditions;

- reward them with a good basic salary and/or an excellent commission structure;

- acknowledge their efforts and achievements;

- be a good manager.

Poor sales people also tend to move around. If you have poor sales people, find out the reason for their lack of performance (lack of training, lack of incentive, etc.) and remedy it. Possibly you hired the wrong person, in which case allow them to move on.

HOW CAN I GET MORE CLIENTS?

The best way to get more clients is to use your key resource, which is your telesales team. Approach the key individual/s in companies similar to those already using the services, and work on them. If you already have companies on board who are happy with the service you are providing, it will be easy to gain recommendations. Ask your existing clients to give you names of contacts in companies they deal with, to approach for work. Other ways could be:

- local and national newspaper and magazine advertising;

- local radio advertising;

- scanning magazines, leaflets, radio ads, etc. so that you know who is spending money on advertising – you can then approach them with the better service you can offer.

As in any business, an important promotional aspect is word of mouth. Therefore, probably the most important source of promotion you can have is to deliver **excellent** service to the clients you already have.

HOW MANY CALLS SHOULD A TELESALES EXECUTIVE MAKE IN AN HOUR? A DAY? A WEEK?

How long is a piece of string? There is no finite answer to this question. While it is reasonable to expect a minimum number of calls from each teleseller, the number of calls made will depend on many different things, for example, the time taken to reach the essential person, the type of product or service being sold. Therefore the minimum number of calls expected from each teleseller will only be properly estimated by an effective manager based on experience.

Top telesales executives will make maximum sales from a minimum of calls. Less effective personnel will accomplish similar sales figures by making more calls. The point at which a good manager needs to become very involved is when any telesales executive is failing to produce sufficient sales despite high levels of telephone calls, sufficient training and regular attendance.

WHERE ELSE CAN I GO FOR ADVICE AND INFORMATION ON EFFECTIVE TELESALES?

At the back of this book, you will find information on other books, websites and organisations related to the field of telesales. These may offer further assistance.

WHY DO PEOPLE SAY THAT THE FIRST FEW SECONDS OF A TELEPHONE CALL ARE THE MOST IMPORTANT?

First impressions are always important. Practise this for yourself. Walk down the street or sit in a coffee bar and notice the people you meet or see. Be aware of the opinions you very quickly form about each person. You will notice that within less than 20 seconds you have probably decided something about each one which would have a strong bearing on your subsequent interaction with them. The next time you answer the telephone, monitor your feelings as you hear the other person's voice. You will find that within the first few seconds you have either warmed to that person or felt rejectful of further communication. There are many books that cover this aspect of human interaction and reaction which is highly pertinent to any sales person who wishes to increase his or her levels of positive response from others.

HOW DO I GET MY TELESALES PERSONNEL TO INCREASE THEIR SALES VOLUME?

First, re-read this book. Secondly, apply what you have learnt. Hire only quality personnel and make sure they are competently trained on the products you are trying to sell. Always encourage them to ask questions and then to ask more questions in order to truly establish the potential client's needs and wants. Make sure they are listening to the responses they receive. Look after your personnel using excellent managerial skills and treat them as professionals. All things being equal, spend time with each and do not allow personal problems to cloud their enthusiasm and initiative.

I AM JUST SETTING UP. WHO DO I CALL?

Call the people with whom you want to do business. Call those who will have a need for your products or services. At the back of this book, you will find details of companies that will supply you with telephone numbers for your target audience.

MY TELESALES EXECUTIVES RECEIVE A LOT OF NEGATIVE RESPONSE. I UNDERSTAND THAT OFTEN PEOPLE BECOME FED UP WITH RECEIVING TELESALES CALLS, BUT HOW CAN I HELP?

You must ensure that good communication is being practised. Part of good communication is being able to gauge if the intended recipient is ready and willing to receive your communication. From a telesales executive's point of view, this translates into making sure that they are calling at an appropriate time. Why waste time and potential clients by calling at inconvenient times? Another thing you, as manager, must see to is that your personnel are calling only qualified potential clients. It may not be possible to fully qualify them without speaking to them first. Therefore, ensure that at the very least they fit into the general category of people or businesses that would be likely to be interested in your product/s or service/s.

HOW DO I, AS MANAGER, COMPETE WITH OTHER FORMS OF MARKETING SUCH AS DIRECT MAIL, E-MAIL, LEAFLETING AND THE INTERNET?

There certainly are many media competing for attention these days. This is where your skill as manager will come into its own. A keynote of your job is to make your business and the message you are putting across worth listening to. Whatever your potential clients, they are not stupid and can tell the difference between amateur attempts at marketing and a worthwhile product or service.

All forms of marketing have their place but one of the most direct, cost-effective and immediate ways to reach people is the telephone. You can of course enhance your own message using direct mail, e-mail and any other form of marketing.

WHERE CAN I PURCHASE GOOD TELEPHONE EQUIPMENT?

There is a very wide range of equipment available from British Telecom and the BT shops. Telephones, headsets and other tools can also be obtained from many high street stores and some of the smaller electrical outlets. Desks, proper seating and other office equipment is readily available from many stores and office equipment suppliers. Many towns will also have warehouses that supply used office equipment if this suits your budget better.

WHAT ABOUT THE LEGAL SIDE OF THINGS?

If your company or business does not have its own legal department, make sure you consult an appropriate solicitor. This will help ensure you are operating within correct legal guidelines. If you don't wish to consult a solicitor, you can approach one of the many business advisory bodies or your local Small Business Bureau.

WHY SHOULDN'T I SIMPLY HAVE MY PERSONNEL WORK THROUGH TELEPHONE DIRECTORIES INSTEAD OF GOING TO MORE COSTLY LENGTHS TO OBTAIN TELEPHONE NUMBERS OF POSSIBLE PROSPECTS?

Professionalism in this competitive field demands that we take all possible measures to fully qualify our prospects. Very few products or services will appeal to everyone in the telephone book. While the telephone directory provides a seemingly endless list of numbers to call, it tells you nothing else about the individual, business or activity and therefore can prove to be very wasteful of your resources.

ARE THERE TECHNIQUES MY PERSONNEL CAN USE TO GET PAST COMPANY RECEPTIONISTS AND MAKE DIRECT CONTACT WITH THE KEY INDIVIDUALS WITHIN A COMPANY?

Receptionists and secretaries have an essential duty to protect their managers from people and situations that are distracting and irrelevant. A professional telesales executive needs to be able to explain how the product or service they are selling can be beneficial to the company or manager they are attempting to reach. Courtesy, amity and brevity are the keynotes of this activity.

HOW CAN I KEEP MY CALL CHARGES TO A MINIMUM?

Shop around. There are many telecommunications suppliers in some areas. In others, these may be limited. Find out about the suppliers in your area.

- Negotiate the best deal you can. If you have some idea (and you should have) of the amounts of calls you are going to be making, you should be able to get an improved rate.

- Have a clear policy on the use of company's telephones for personal use.

- Train your personnel to recognise that the length of time spent on one call is not necessarily reflected in sales.

- If your potential clients can be just as easily contacted in off-peak hours, and it is feasible to do so, leave the bulk of your telephone calls for those times.

THERE SEEM TO BE MANY COMPANIES USING THE TELEPHONE, LEAFLETS, E-MAIL AND DIRECT MAIL THAT COMPETITION IS VERY HIGH. HOW DO I KNOW MY TELESALES BUSINESS WILL SUCCEED?

Any successful business man will tell you that it is a professional attitude and competence coupled with a drive to succeed towards clear goals that matters. The telephone is the most successful and important tool in today's business world. Use it properly and make it work for you. Use the guidelines in this book and you will be well on the way to winning!

I DON'T LIKE RECEIVING TELESALES CALLS MYSELF. DOES THIS MEAN I'M A HYPOCRITE?

Not at all. You can, however, use the telesales calls you receive personally and which annoy you to work out for yourself what it is you didn't like about the call:

- Did you receive the call at an inconvenient time?

- Was the person obviously reading from a script?

- Was their tone too personal or impersonal?

- Were you talked at or were you asked questions?

- Was the product or service being sold relevant to your needs?

- What impression did you build of the caller?

- Was the caller courteous?

SOME TELESALES COMPANIES EMPLOY A MEANS OF VERIFYING THE VALIDITY OF SUCH THINGS AS APPOINTMENTS MADE, SALES ORDER AND START DATES. DOESN'T THIS UNDERMINE THE TELESALES EXECUTIVES?

If you decide to utilise one of your personnel to do this, as long as it is made clear to all your staff there should be no problem. Broken appointments, cancelled orders and start dates being changed are problems that have to be kept to a minimum. If, as manager, you keep all informed about changes to company's policy and any reasons why, no one is undermined at all.

WHAT IS THE MOST IMPORTANT THING TO REMEMBER AS (A) A TELESALES EXECUTIVE, (B) A MANAGER?

Don't worry too much about remembering things. What is important is what you and your personnel **do**. Here are some important **dos**:

- Do employ staff with good communication skills and a friendly approach.

- Do provide professional working conditions.

- Do call only qualified prospects.

- Do have goals and work towards them.

- Do ensure your staff come to work properly fed having had sufficient sleep and ready for work.

- Do insist upon courtesy to potential clients and each other.

- Do listen to your staff and make sure they are listening to the people they are calling.

- Do demand achievement and reward it when it is attained.

- Do continue to expand upon your skills and knowledge in this field and expect your personnel to do the same.

WHAT ABOUT ALL THE VARIOUS SALES GIMMICKS?

There are many different 'sales tricks' and 'gimmicks' around. There always will be. However, many of these are simply methods that have worked for one or two individuals. This does not mean they will work for everyone. They should not necessarily be embraced as the only way to get things done.

14

Looking to the Future

> 'They (the great managers) are the ones who recognise problems, seize opportunities, and create their own future. Ultimately, they are the ones who stop to think where they want to go and then have the shameless audacity to set out.'
>
> (Gerard M. Blair)

The future of the telesales industry is very bright. With more and more companies cutting back on expensive field sales representation, and the fax, telephone, e-mail, Internet and e-commerce in general becoming more and more popular because of its speed, we have much to look forward to.

EVER INCREASING COMPETITION

There is one problem to face, however. The telephone lines of the world are growing at a rate never before seen because of the expansion of e-commerce and the Internet. This means, of course, that increasingly more and more companies will be utilising telesales departments to gain business and to keep business in an ever-increasingly competitive way. So what is the problem? Keeping hold of your share of the market!

We are going to have to keep ahead of the rest of the field in order to make our businesses stay profitable and this means diligence and hard work. Nevertheless, it means that we are going to have to be the best we can be. Professionalism will be the byword of tomorrow's telesales industry. If we can't be professional – and as professional as we can be – we will not survive the growing competition.

KEYNOTES FOR SURVIVAL

The keynotes of survival in tomorrow's telephone sales industry will be as they have always been:

- communication skills;
- listening skills;
- qualifying, qualifying and qualifying prospects;
- being as professional as you can be.

Offering the right product or service to the right person in the right company, and not wasting time and effort in attempting to sell something that is inappropriate to someone who does not and will not have a need for it, will be crucial in tomorrow's competitive world of sales. Hit and miss 'shotgun' approaches in telesales and its rival direct mail will continue, no doubt, to be used, but will become less effective than calls and mailings to fully qualified prospects.

THE MANAGEMENT PHILOSOPHY FOR THE FUTURE

Although some companies continue to practise a dinosaur management or personnel philosophy ('make your target or you are sacked'), there will be no place for such an outlook within the telesales and telemarketing world of the future. Training, personnel skills and an adept approach to personnel motivation will be the essential features of the skilled and successful telesales manager of tomorrow, as they are already becoming today.

It seems that wherever one looks today, there is an abundance of material, in every media, on all the important subjects involved in modern management and production. Therefore there is no excuse for any manager to fail to move forwards and take his or her unit, branch or company to the very highest levels of success.

THE TECHNOLOGY OF TOMORROW

In Chapter 8 we looked at some of the current innovations in project tracking and software for telesales and telemarketing. Have no doubt that this side of telesales administration will continue forward in leaps and bounds, making paper-based telesales offices outdated. Aside from anything else, such systems provide rapidity of information flow way beyond paper-based systems, and providing that their personnel are competent and professional, offices utilising such systems will be at the head of the field.

A FINAL WORD

There are many aspects of telesales and telemarketing and their management which we have not looked at in this book. There are only so many things that one can advise others upon – the rest must be left up to the personal initiative and creativity of the managers themselves.

> Use this book to help make your telesales and tele-marketing dreams and goals a reality!

Glossary

Business-to-business. Sales activity and commerce from one company to another

Cold call. An initial telephone call to establish the status of any potential customer. A call which may or may not yield any positive results

Commitment. Commitment is doing or providing what you said you would, although the incentive or mood that was present at the time may have passed.

DMA. The Direct Marketing Association.

Goals. Goals are what we are aiming for. They may be short, medium or long term objectives which are always our final destination.

H&SE. Health and Safety Executive – a government body that issues guidelines designed to increase health and safety in the workplace, among other things.

Headset. A telephone mouthpiece and earpiece which clips over the head.

Listening. Listening is being consciously aware of what another is saying to you. Where sales is concerned, we can also say that listening includes a commercial awareness (being aware of opportunities to forward the product or service you are selling).

Motivation. The desire, interest and determination to move in a given direction or focus one's attention.

OFTEL. The Office of Telecommunications.

Proactive. Deciding what to do, working out how to do it, and doing it; encouraging others to do the same.

Product. That item or service which is produced and has value to another.

Project tracking. Any system whereby the progress of a project can be monitored. Project tracking systems allow not only the progress of the project to be monitored, but facilitate various reports and contact details to be recorded also.

Prospect. Any individual or individual within a company who may use your products or services.

Qualified. We say a prospect is qualified when it has been established that they have: (a) a desire, need or use for the product or service we wish to sell them and, (b) they have the resources to pay for such a product or service.

Reactive. Responding to a stimulus in the surroundings.

Script. Any written text that is designed to act as a prompt or information sheet for use by telesales personnel.

Target. A target is a specified amount of a given product to be produced.

Telephone image. How the person at the other end of your telephone call perceives you.

Telesales. The telephone promotion of goods and services. This can be directed towards both commercial and residential prospects.

Telesales executive. Any professional who uses the telephone as his or her main tool to sell products or services.

TPS. Telephone Preference Scheme – a scheme that gives the public the right to protection in their homes from the intrusion of direct marketing telephone calls.

Training. Demonstrating, teaching or showing how something is to be done with the result that the person trained can then carry out the task to good effects.

Further Reading

Books about telesales are available in bookshops and via the Internet and there are many of them. However most do not just specialise in telesales but also look at such subjects as networking, field sales and other aspects of the sales business. Some of the books you may wish to read are listed here.

The successful manager's guide to business-to-business telephone sales operations, Lee R. Van Vechten. (Business by phone Inc. 1999).

Managing through people, John Humphries. (How To Books 1998). An interesting guide to management of personnel.

The one-minute manager, D. Kenneth blanchard (Blanchard and Johnson 1982). Is the first of a series of books that looks at concise ways in which management can be developed, and is strongly recommended for any manager in any field.

TalkWorks – How to get more out of life through better conversations, Andrew Bailey and Gerard Egan (British Telecommunications plc 1999). Covers the subject of communication both generally and in depth, it is alone in its class. Far too few books cover the subject of communication and conversation. This one should be an invaluable study, not just for telesales personnel and managers, for whom it should be mandatory reading, but also for everyone.

Other books on the subject of telemarketing and telesales and using the telephone include:

Telephone Techniques, Lin Walker (Marshall Publishing 1999). Offers an excellent overview of different methods to improve telephone professionalism, but is not telesales specific. It is a very useful book for anyone using the telephone as part of their job, from receptionists/telephonists to customer service personnel.

The Telesales Pocketbook, The Sales and Marketing Series, Peter Wyllie (Stylus Publishing 1999). Advises the reader about increasing sales volume through the telephone. The book goes into complaints ever the telephone and the best ways to work with both incoming and outgoing calls.

Useful Addresses

The following may be of some use in providing information on matters mentioned in this book:

Kaymex Consultants (Sales and Marketing), Making words work for you and your business. Effective Sales and Marketing Solutions. 75 Courtland Road, Chelston, Torquay, Devon TQ2 6JS. Tel: 01803 392107. Email: kaymex@inyan.netlineuk.net
Contact: Stephen Kaye

Woodrow Personal Development Services, 1, Church Road, Newton Abbot, Devon TW12 1AL. Tel/Fax: 01626 333382. Email: woodrodev@aol.com
Training, Consultation, Coaching and Counselling.
Contact: Mr Ian Woodrow

The Telephone Preference Service. Tel: 01932 414161. *www.dataprotection.gov.uk*
Here you can find out exactly what the Telephone Preference Service is and how to best make use of it.

Oftel (Office of Telecommunicatons): Consumer Representation Compliance Directorate, 50 Ludgate Hill, London, EC4M 7JJ. Direct Line: (020) 7634 5305. Lo-Call: 0845 7145000. Fax: (020) 7634 8845 Website: *www.oftel.gov.uk*

There are numerous websites around the world, which offer advice and guidance on telesales and management.

www.tsuccess.dircon.co.uk
An interesting web site offering a range of information as well as training courses for managers and telesales personnel.

www.businessbyphone.com
Another useful web site, in which visitors can exchange their views and comments and ask questions. A wealth of material

is available here for the professional manager and telesales executive alike. Some cost may be involved.

Thomson Directories Ltd, Thomson House, 296 Farnborough Road, Farnborough, Hants, GU14 7NU. Tel: 01252 555555. Web site: *www.thomweb.co.uk*
With information on over 2 million UK businesses, whether you are in sales, marketing or customer services, Thomson Directories can be an invaluable tool.

www.scoot.co.uk
A useful web site for businesses.

British Telecom Business Customer Services. Tel: 152.

Yellow Pages. Tel: 01753 550079.

Index

Printed in Great Britain
by Amazon.co.uk, Ltd.,
Marston Gate.